# PARENTING
# THE LEAN WAY

*Business Inspired Solutions for
Empowering the Family*

"The way in which Jared creatively uses business principles/ examples and applies them to a family setting is incredible. A very helpful guide on how to deal with the people you love. I highly recommend it."

Manuel Trigo, CEO NextPlayers.mx, Mexico

"Inspiring and mind opening. A manual for personal life relationships that nobody should miss! Jared Thatcher talks straight to the heart of real interpersonal relationship problems with a wise yet funny and delightful way. A profoundly easy, direct and unpretentious read, which tackles some of our biggest challenges in a surprisingly pleasant and deeply educational way."

Despoina Kentrou, Finance, Greece

"Loved the idea of bringing and applying powerful business tools to family matters. As a marketing professional, chapter ten caught my attention as it speaks of family brand management. It is certainly true, you have to know what your values are, and what you stand for, to know who you are and where are you heading. A truly inspiring book and a practical guide for families who want to make a difference in their lives."

Lorena Romero, Marketing Executive, Panama

"A good guide for any parent who wants to imbibe good discipline, commitment, while fostering children with great values that will positively affect society. The book will no doubt be very useful to parents with great minds and, most importantly, it will help in nurturing godly children."

Harrison Mordi Williams, Banker, Nigeria

"Jared's parenting concepts are like looking through the family relationship with a different lens that can give you clearer solutions for your family."

Krischasorn "Dee" Udomwadhanaphorn, Deputy Executive Director at Petroleum Institute of Thailand, Thailand

"Great ideas on how to use advanced business tools like lean management and value analysis in our family life. I believe this book will be useful not only in helping with our personal lives, but also improving our understanding and usage of these business tools in our work life."

Nurjan Nurjanov, Husband, Father, and Financial Controller, Turkmenistan

"The author is a pioneer in employing business tools to serve family situations, creating this hand-book that can be a daily reference for better parenting. This book brings a new thinking to the wisdom of parenting presented in a well-structured guidance, written in a user-friendly language with key messages clearly highlighted for ease of reference. The quotes included have added to the value of the book, raised its importance and emphasized the relevance of its unique business based program to family life. Reading this book has been an absolute pleasure. Every sentence is an ongoing living situation for any parent and can earn a smile or put you in deep thoughts – *a must-read for every parent.*"

Molham Shurbaji, Father, Architect, Scotland

"I have been able to read your book and truly find it very helpful and educational. I am confident this book will unlock minds."

Solomon Okopi, Father, Farmer, and former Banker, Nigeria

"Your book is *absolutely astonishing!*"

"The secret of parenting is something that dads and moms are eager to learn. If you are a business professional that understands the "lean concept", then you are already a parent that holds the key to a blissful family. Read the book and you too will know how to unlock it."

"*A book that should be given to every parent!* Rich, thoughtful and practical. Written with a pen but with the depth of Jared's humble heart."

# PARENTING THE LEAN WAY

*Business Inspired Solutions for Empowering the Family*

by

## JARED E. THATCHER

**Parenting the Lean Way:** Business Inspired Solution for Empowering the Family

©2017 by Jared E. Thatcher

Cover Design by germancreative on Fiverr.com
Photos by 123rf.com on pages 25, 146, 214 – 219
Photos by stocksunlimited.com on pages 220, 221
Photos by graphicstock.com on page 222, 233
Photos by author on pages 101, 112, 225
Copy of advertisement on page 57 provided by Jaguar Land Rover North America, LLC.

Published by FamilyMBA Press a division of Thatcher & Company, LLC.
Printed by CreateSpace, Charleston, SC
Facebook Page: fb.me/ParentingTheLeanWay
Book Website: www.parentingtheleanway.com
FamilyMBA can schedule the author for your live event or private coaching. For more information or to book an event visit www.familymba.com

ISBN 978-0-9991424-0-0 Paperback
ISBN 978-0-9991424-1-7 eBook

SPECIAL SALES
FamilyMBA Press has available exclusive discounts for bulk purchases for sales promotions or custom special editions. Special editions, including personalized covers, excerpts of this book, and corporate imprints, can be created in large quantities for special needs. For more information, write to: marketing@familymba.com

# Dedication

*To my beautiful wife who saw how the tools I was using in the business world could help us at home and supported me in developing these concepts.*

*To my wonderful children who have humored me as I applied these concepts into their lives.*

*To my parents who exemplify the traits of what parents should be.*

*To the parents everywhere who want to provide a better life for their children and are willing to try new things to help their families grow closer together.*

*I love you all.*

# CONTENTS

# INTRODUCTION

## Parents Need a Competitive Edge
## (the Kids Certainly Won't Give it to Us)

*Business tools can be used to transform yourself, your family, and your kids. Using these tools and Lean methodology you can transform your family into that ideal future state you always wished was possible.*

The other day, I had an experience that perhaps some of you can relate to. As I was taking my daughter to preschool, I saw a mom dropping off her kids. She looked as though she was practically in tears. As we both headed back to our cars, I could hear her mutter under her breath, "I can't wait to get to work." I'm sure we've all had days like that.

Why is it that work can seem less stressful than running a home? Perhaps it's because at work there are systems in place that eliminate some of the chaos that we experience at home. We can see solutions easier at work from 'outside the box' because we are not as emotionally invested. Our emotional connection to our family sometimes makes it harder to see solutions as clearly. This book is designed to help you see solutions from 'inside the box.'

## What is Parenting the Lean Way?

Parenting the Lean Way increases the tools we have available in our parenting tool box by using the business philosophy of Lean. In business or parenting, Lean can make life easier. In its simplest form, Lean changes your focus from you to those you serve. Lean looks for ways to increase the value of what you do for others, while eliminating or reducing those things that are not adding value. Continuous improvement is at the heart of Lean. It can help you manage your time, improve your ability to communicate, solve problems, resolve conflicts, and exhibit leadership. The Lean Way can be used by parents to improve family life.

Over the last few decades new research and innovations in the business world, and other industries like education and government, have all developed transformative tools and methods to improve some of these areas of life. These ideas are kept primarily "in-house". They are not shared outside of their sphere of influence where they were conceived. This is a shame. These ideas can have the greatest impact for good within our families not only where they originated.

In a business context, these tools are typically seen as unemotional and logical. When used in a family context with love and concern, these business tools transform into compassionate instruments any parent would feel comfortable using to help their family. My purpose is to share these fresh ideas and tools with you and your family to help you achieve stronger family relationships.

These tools provide a way to look at situations from a unique perspective. They can help us make informed decisions. Clarity increases. Mutually beneficial solutions are reached. The quality of our communication increases. Satisfaction in your family relationships will be at an all-time high. A shift from reactionary parenting to proactive parenting is achieved. Solutions to conflicts become clearer. Accountability for modifying behavior is created. Character building values and beliefs become part of your family's core. Parenting the Lean Way empowers your family to work together to improve your individual lives and family relationships.

Applying these business tools will pay tremendous dividends to you as a parent. These tools and techniques will empower you and your family to achieve goals. Accountability for making positive improvements will become second nature. Visual management will reduce or eliminate the need to nag. Your children will proactively work to solve problems, because you will provide them with the latitude to gain their own independence. By using these tools, you will know your family members better, and be looking for ways to help them have the best experiences they can have.

Parenting the Lean Way is about taking the journey together as a family to be the best you can be. My family and I have used the tools and methods shared in this book with great success. I also teach these tools on a regular basis to parents and their children.

Surprisingly enough, it is often the children who embrace and use these tools with greater enthusiasm than their parents, due to the empowerment that it gives them. To illustrate practical applications of some of these tools, I share personal stories from my own family's experiences with their permission. Other families have also graciously agreed to share their success stories.

## How Parenting the Lean Way Began

Several years ago, I was involved in a global change management initiative at work. The company wanted to change the culture within the organization. The desire of management was to encourage the office employees to implement Lean principles into their daily work. Several of my colleagues and myself were chosen to work alongside McKinsey consultants to teach the Lean philosophy, tools, and methodology to all the departments in the company.

Every day I would come home eager to tell my wife about the fantastic results we were having integrating Lean across the company. The teams I worked with did a complete 180° turn, as they both worked together and communicated better. Thanks to these Lean tools, we were positively impacting the morale of the departments. We were strengthening the leadership and coaching abilities of the managers. Processes and systems were being continuously improved upon, which led to millions of dollars being saved as a result of those improvements. I loved what I was doing. I was making a real difference in the company, especially in the work lives of my colleagues.

One evening, as I returned home anxious to share the latest success story I had from work, my wife was waiting for me just inside the door with her hands on her hips. This is never a good sign. I quickly tried to remember if I had forgotten an anniversary, or to do something she had asked me to do. Much to my relief, that was not it at all. My wife informed me that she was completely exhausted after an especially long day. The boys had been arguing; and our daughter, who at the time was about a year old, had single-handedly created a tornado that had displaced every toy in the house. My wife needed my help desperately.

"Jared, couldn't you take the things that you learned in your MBA, and the cool things you're doing at work, and use them to help our family?" she implored.

Instantly, I saw two separate circles forming a Venn diagram in my mind. One circle represented family, the other represented work. As soon as my wife posed her question, I had an epiphany. I realized that I had compartmentalized work and family into two separate areas of my life.

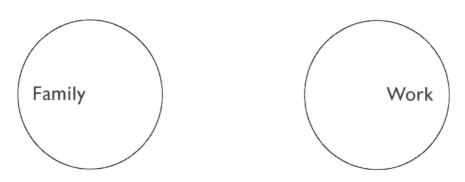

As the Venn diagram came crashing together in my mind, revealing the intersecting commonality, I realized that many of the things I was doing at work could indeed help my family. I accepted her challenge. I was going to figure out what I could take from work to help our family.

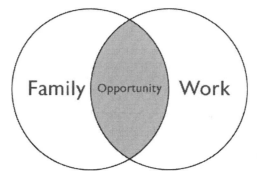

For the last several years, I have been looking for the best business inspired solutions and soft-skill development tools the business world has to offer. I took the question my wife asked and have been tailoring these business tools specifically for family situations. After extensive testing and numerous family workshops, I am happy to share what I call "Parenting the Lean Way."

**What is Lean?**

What exactly is Lean? It is a business concept from the manufacturing world that mandates that your focus should always be on your customer's needs (the value and quality they expect). Most of the tools of Lean are thus focused on the continuous improvement of work processes. They systematically increase the quality and value you provide to your customer, while eliminating what doesn't provide the customer with any value. This non-value-added work we refer to as waste. Lean then is a methodology of continuous improvement to add value for the customer, while reducing or eliminating waste from the system. I'll share more on the history and principles of Lean in the next couple chapters.

As I share strategies and tools I have learned as a father, a husband, a business consultant, and through the workshops I have been teaching, I know these will be of value to you and your family and make your home and personal life easier. The concepts in this book are not new ones. These are proven strategies used by millions of people in the business world. Many of these people are successfully using these concepts and tools in their own personal and home life as well. These tools in this book can make as positive a difference in your family as they have in mine.

You are going to find your parenting toolbox grow with these innovative and practical solutions to help your family. While these tools are business inspired solutions, they are to be used with love, empathy, and concern. When used in this way, you will find they will empower your family to draw closer together, and your children will gain confidence that will prepare them for their future as independent, capable adults.

Just because these tools are rooted in business, does not mean I am suggesting you run your home like a business. Nor am I suggesting you use these tools to create mindless worker drones to serve corporations. Rather, these tools simply provide a uniquely straightforward way for dealing with problems. They strengthen the executive functioning skills that we all need to learn to be well-rounded individuals.

**How Will Business Tools Help Me with Parenting?**

The tools you will learn in Parenting the Lean Way will provide you with that competitive edge in your parenting skills to stay actively engaged with your children. It will get you on the same page to achieve family goals together. You will learn how to get to the root cause of problems so that you are fixing the issues, rather than the symptoms. Your example will teach leadership skills to your children, so that they will be empowered by you to critically think and solve their own problems. This will not only increase their confidence, but it will also help them gain a real advantage in life.

I've always had a passion for wanting to be a better parent, even before I became one. In high school, I first noticed a correlation between classmates who were getting into trouble and their home life. Specifically, their relationships with their parents. I resolved at that early age that I was going to learn what worked well and apply it when I became a parent.

Of course, when I became a parent, I realized that what works well for one child, might not impact another. Every child is different. Every situation is unique. Despite my best efforts, I don't always get it right. And that's okay. My children know beyond a doubt that my wife and I love them unconditionally, and that makes up for the times when I get it wrong. I'm always trying to improve.

I am so pleased that you are willing to take this journey to better parenting with me. It truly is a journey. An exploration into uncharted territory might be a better description. The ideas I will be presenting are unique among parenting courses. I've consulted with numerous parenting and family experts about using business tools to help the family. While many do use some of these tools, none have created a training based entirely on business tools and methods.

It's interesting that parenting books will refer to using business tools to help in parenting, and business books will likewise refer to the application of their tools at home. Yet, no one has gathered up these tools and frameworks into one resource to help parents and children. In that regard, this truly is an innovative parenting course. True innovation has the power to take you from where you are, to someplace you never imagined you could go.

Using business tools to help the family makes perfect sense. Think about it, businesses worldwide spend hundreds of billions of dollars every year to train employees[i] and improve the bottom line. Foremost in that training is how to improve the "Soft Skills" of the employees. Leadership, teamwork, effective communications, time management, problem solving, conflict resolution, coaching and mentoring skills are all areas that have just as much impact at home as they do at work. As important as these skills are to help us in our parenting, it is even more important that we teach these soft skills to our children.

You might be thinking, that businesses and families have nothing in common. But please, think again.

Families constitute the largest manufacturing cottage industry in the world. Where else can you take unskilled laborers and have them produce the most complex and innovative product imaginable? . . . Children!

As a parent, you spend the first eighteen years of a child's life trying to refine, reshape, and influence that perfect product in an endeavor to prepare them to be self-sufficient adults. Ultimately, our adult children will be the product of our parenting.

### Teaching Children Business Tools to Prepare them for Life

As your children learn these soft skills, they will gain a competitive edge in their academics. As they enter the workforce, they will have developed the problem solving and leadership skills necessary to give them a competitive edge in their careers. When they become parents themselves, they will be able to raise their children in a way that will make you proud of the job they are doing. You will be giving them a great gift by teaching them how to apply the skills found in this book.

I first noticed how business concepts can influence our children almost fifteen years ago. My eldest son was almost four when he had his first and only grocery store meltdown. The dreaded meltdown. He asked for something, we said no, and the temper tantrum to end all tantrums began. I picked him up and walked with my screaming son out to the parking lot, while my wife stayed to complete the shopping.

In the car, I calmly explained to my son that if he ever fussed or behaved like that again, the answer would always be no. When he had calmed down a little bit, I asked him to restate to me what I had told him. He did. He appeared to have learned his lesson. And to be fair to him, he had never behaved that way before or since that time.

But then I made a mistake I have come to regret. I taught my son a business sales closing technique. It is a simple assumption close. You assume the person will buy what you are selling. You give them two choices other than yes or no. Do you want this car in the standard black, or would you prefer it in blue? Shall we meet in the morning or would the afternoon be more convenient?

I also explained again to my son a rule we have in our family. If we as the parents ever give an answer that they don't like, they are allowed one chance to explain to us why we should reconsider. They only get one chance. This forces them to think. To provide us with additional information, which might cause us to change our minds.

I didn't think that our conversation had much of an impact until several months later. We were again at a grocery store, when I see my son coming down the aisle with a package of chocolate cupcakes in one hand and vanilla cupcakes in the other. I knew I was in trouble.

With a twinkle in his eye, he said, "Dad, remember how you said we could make some treats when we get home?"

"Yes." I answered hesitatively, waiting to see where this was going.

"Well, when we get home it will be too late to make treats, and I'll have to go to bed. . . So, do you want the vanilla cupcakes, or the chocolate cupcakes?"

Lesson learned!

"Both!" I said, as his eyes grew as big as his smile.

That was a simple business sales tool. He learned it at a young age. It has served him well. He learned not to argue, but to make a good case (most of the time). To look at it from the other's perspective. To present multiple options to choose from, instead of a simple yes or no answer.

There are thousands of potential tools like these that we could use as parents to teach our children, to help them grow up to be independent and self-sufficient adults. As a parent, the concepts in this book apply to you no matter what kind of a parent you are. Single, married, divorced, separated, or even if you haven't started a family yet, it doesn't matter. If you are interested in learning a few new tools to add to your parenting toolbox, then this book is for you.

In this book, I will present you with a couple of dozen business tools that will positively impact you and your family. I will also capitalize the names of these tools throughout this book, so that they jump off the page as you are reading them.

### How this Book is Organized

I have divided this book up into three sections. Section One lays the foundation of what Lean is and some of the principles behind this business philosophy.

Chapter 1 cover the history of Lean by examining the power of ideas.

Chapter 2 lays the foundation behind the Lean Way by understanding four of the main principles of Lean.

Chapters 3 – 4 discuss two pivotal elements of the Lean Way, the concepts of Value and Waste.

Chapter 5 wraps up the first part of the book by revealing the crown jewel of the business tools that will help your family – The Family Board.

Section Two dives deeply into the five phases of the GATES™ framework, which I teach in my family workshops to help families continuously improve.

Chapter 6 provides an overview of the GATES™ framework, while Chapter 7 discusses tools on how to overcome change resistance you might experience with your family.

Chapters 8 – 10 address tools to help **G**ATHER ideas to strengthen your family, provide a strong moral foundation that you establish, and to identify areas for improvement.

Chapters 11 – 13 show you how to **A**SK the right questions to identify the root cause(s) of a problem and solve it once and for all, rather than trying to fix symptoms (which can leave you wondering why things never get any better).

Chapters 14 and 15 will help you **T**INKER around at making the solutions happen using visual management and a project and time management tool – the Mini Sprint™.

Chapter 16 is all about the **E**XPERIMENT you will do in testing your solution(s) to see if they work, by tracking your results through Key Performance Indicators (KPIs).

Chapters 17 and 18 rounds off the GATES™ portion of the system by showing you how to **S**USTAIN the improvements your family has made so that you don't backslide and lose those gains.

Finally, Section Three is simply the conclusion to the concepts found in the Lean Way.

Chapter 19 concludes by summarizing everything and providing a glimpse into what the future holds for Parenting the Lean Way.

You are in the right place. If you find yourself not happy and satisfied with the way you respond when family members push your buttons; if you wish that your children got along better with you and their siblings; if you want your family to communicate better; if you wish to increase your children's problem solving skills; if you wish you could improve the quality and quantity of time you spend together as a family; and most importantly, if you wish you could reduce the stress that you feel as a parent – *then Parenting the Lean Way is for you.*

Let's embark together on this incredible journey of empowering our families. I'm excited you have decided to join me on this journey to Parenting the Lean Way.

> *"Convince a man of what he wants,*
> *and he will move heaven and earth to get it."*
> *- Anonymous*

# SECTION 1:

## *The Foundation*

# CHAPTER 1

## The Power of Ideas –
## How a Question Can
## Inspire Your Parenting

*You never know where an idea will come from. The power of all great ideas comes from asking the right questions. To best help your family, what questions do you need to ask yourself?*

L et's explore the power of ideas – specifically, the power of business ideas. After all, this book is about translating those business ideas into tools and systems that can benefit you at home or at work.

This chapter is here to provide you with the context of how Lean came to be. It also is designed to reinforce the concept that all great ideas that have changed the world, came from someone asking a question to solve a problem. The point of this chapter is to reveal the contextual background of Lean and inspire you to never stop questioning things, because your inquiry might spark an idea that could change your family or the world. If you want to skip this chapter because you want to get to the concepts and tools behind the Lean Way, I understand.

Businesses are interested in improving performance, team work, communications, marketing, processes, and of course, the bottom line or profit. It really is no surprise to find that worldwide companies spend over $300 billion a year on training their employees[ii]. Firms have paid consultants, psychologists, efficiency experts, and university professors billions of dollars to develop simple systems for their employees to learn better ways to solve problems, improve employee team working skills, streamline processes, and generate more sales and profit. Why not learn from some of these tools and systems they have developed for work and apply them at home?

The power of ideas comes from recognizing a problem or an obstacle and then figuring out a way to solve the problem. There have been fantastic inventions that have transformed the world all based on a single idea. The cotton-gin, the steam engine, and even Thomas Edison's light bulb. Did you realize that after the invention of the light bulb, Edison had to invent and create power plants and the power grid to generate the electricity necessary to power the light bulbs? Talk about impressive.

But one of the greatest inventions from the last century was Henry Ford's assembly line. Ford wanted to produce more cars. Making vehicles faster would bring down the cost of the automobile, thereby making it affordable to the average person. When Ford built conveyor belts and gravity feed tracks to move things around to the workers, the assembly line was born. This revolutionary idea to improve how quickly a car was made, came about because he wanted to lower the cost and make it more affordable.

How much was Ford able to lower the cost based on this production innovation? The price went from $800 down to just $300 per vehicle!

The power of an idea has the ability to transform the world; Ford's assembly line did just that! Ford's innovation transformed the lives of families around the world by providing a means of effectively and efficiently producing more goods, quicker, and at increasingly cheaper prices. This in turn increased the living standards of hundreds of millions of families. We are the beneficiaries of this manufacturing innovation idea.

Henry Ford with Ford Model T Car, Buffalo, New York 1921. From the Collections of The Henry Ford. Gift of Ford Motor Company.

As fascinating and important as the assembly line was to revolutionizing business, the next business idea I'm going to introduce has been called by some the "third wave" of the industrial revolution. This business idea has simplicity at its core. The idea is known as *Lean*. The official name is the Toyota Production System or TPS for short. The ideas developed from TPS, or Lean, as I will refer to it as in this book, work not just in the business world, but contain some simple principles that will help you as a parent as well.

Before I explain how the business idea of Lean can help you as a parent, I want to make sure that you understand what Lean is. If you've never heard of Lean, that's okay. I'm going to tell you a story about how Lean came to be, and more importantly, what it is.

Simply put, Lean is centered around the concept of continuous improvement. As you will see in the story of how Lean came to be, massive improvements in quality, effectiveness, and efficiency were made. Not by any big improvement or innovation, but by numerous small improvements.

As you learn more about Lean, you will find that there may be areas of your life that need improvement too. If you apply the business concepts and tools which will be discussed in this book, you and your family will benefit from these ideas.

The business idea of Lean was created in Japan by Toyota after the Second World War. On September 2, 1945, Japan had officially surrendered, but its cities and industries were utterly destroyed – especially its manufacturing ability. Japan had a long road ahead to rebuild.

In hopes of improving their own manufacturing process in 1950, Toyota executives took a three-month trip to the US to see how Ford manufactured its cars. At that time, Toyota was producing around 2,500 cars a year; Ford, by contrast, was producing nearly 8,000 cars a day. Ford could produce a car ten times faster than Toyota. And when it came to quality, Toyota wasn't even in the ball park. Ford's quality was thirty times better! Thirty Times! Can you imagine?

One executive, Taiichi Ohno, a plant manager, was charged with getting Toyota's production to compete and equal Ford's production. That was quite a challenge – one that Mr. Ohno would spend the remainder of his life working on.

Taiichi Ohno

He realized that as a company, Toyota didn't have the resources needed to invest in the equipment necessary to produce cars in the same way as Ford. They needed to find a new, less expensive way to compete. He needed an idea.

What he created has been referred to as "the poor man's production system." Today that system is simply known as Lean. In fact, one of the major ideas for improvement on the production floor actually came from a visit to a supermarket while in the United States. Mr. Ohno liked how organized everything was, and how quickly you could find what you were looking for. From that visit and concept, he developed an inventory management system that would change manufacturing around the world. All this developed from watching people using shopping carts. You never know where an idea will come from.

Toyota's big breakthrough came when they asked the question, "How can we increase earnings without raising our prices *and* have our quality increase at the same time?" That's a question that would change the world. Improve quality without raising prices and increase earnings at the same time? That question seems to be in conflict with itself, yet to achieve the answer to that question, Lean manufacturing was born.

As you'll read throughout this book, it's an idea that is going to forever change the way you look at the world. It will help you to improve your family and yourself. How can I make that claim? You'll see soon. But let's continue for a moment with the story. Let's fast forward thirty years to when Toyota took the Western world by surprise.

In 1982, General Motors had a plant in California that it had to close because it was having major problems. It had an absenteeism rate pushing 20%. Can you imagine that on any given day roughly 20% of your workforce didn't even show up?

Two years later Toyota was looking to expand into the U.S. market, and GM was more than happy to work out an arrangement with Toyota to use the plant they had just closed down. GM even warned Toyota not to hire back the old employees. Well, Toyota mostly ignored that advice. They hired back the rank and file "problem" line workers, but did not hire back the managers. Instead, they replaced all of them with their own managers.

What happened? Two years later, in 1986, Toyota showed the world what they had learned over three decades earlier from that initial visit to Ford. In 1986, it took GM 40 hours to produce a car, Toyota could do it in 18 hours. GM had an average of 13 defects per 10 vehicles, compared to Toyota with only 4.5 defects. That's nearly three times fewer defects produced in less than half the time!

And remember that 20% absenteeism rate GM had four years previous? Well, Toyota experienced a 3% absenteeism with those same workers who they hired back. That plant was also voted "Best in Class" for employee satisfaction. What a change! Even more amazing was that the Lean Principles that Toyota used to achieve these results, which I will introduce to you in the next chapter, were taught throughout Japanese industry. It was part of the fundamental reason that Japan could transform itself from a destroyed nation at the end of the war to the second largest economy in the world within roughly twenty years. It's a position they maintained for thirty years until China recently came on the scene.

The power of Lean comes from empowering the workers to solve problems and issues when they see it. Lean is not dependent upon managers to make decisions. Anyone can improve quality for the customer when they see a way to improve a process. Lean is about using small incremental improvements to enhance value and reduce waste.

Lean is now used outside of manufacturing. It is being applied in offices, in health care, in banking, in IT, and even in schools, just to name a few areas. In fact, IT software development has further refined Lean into something known as Agile. In subsequent chapters I will show you some tools which have been developed from Agile as well, that you can use to help your family.

As I just mentioned, the appeal of Lean is that it empowers everyone in an organization to contribute to its betterment. Anyone can identify a problem and solve it. You see an opportunity for improvement, you implement it. The focus of everyone in the organization changes from inward to outward. They focus on the needs of the customer, both internal and external, and they work on ways to improve the value they are providing. Team work increases, and morale improves because of the trust in the workers to proactively take the initiative.

Major companies today are just starting to implement these ideas of Lean into their businesses. I've worked with a multitude of companies, both as an employee and as a management consultant, to implement Lean concepts into their workforce. Companies like Daimler, Nike, Standard Insurance, PGE, and Kimber, to name a few.

Once people learn the principles of Lean, many apply them into their own personal lives and even use it at home. So, while I'm not the first one to apply Lean, or Agile, or other business tools or methods to the family, I believe that I am the first to put it into a training course, so that you too can benefit from it.

As great as this history lesson was about Lean, you are still probably wondering, "What does any of this have to do with me becoming a better parent? I mean, how will this help me improve the communication in my home, or stop the nagging and yelling, or get the kids to do their chores, or even help me feel appreciated?"

If you are thinking that, fair enough. But, here is why you should sit up and take notice. For Lean to be able to transform an actively disengaged, even hostile workforce (whom Toyota rehired), and then turn those same workers into workers ranked "Best in Class" for employee satisfaction – that's beyond huge. This Lean philosophy was even able to help transform Japan after the war into the second largest economy in the world in twenty years. It's truly an unbelievable transformation, that also happens to be about the same amount of time we have as parents to influence our children before they become adults.

Think of what is possible if you or I can learn just a portion of the principles from Lean that produces a change in people's mindset to achieve those kinds of results? With the huge gains in effectiveness, efficiency and worker satisfaction that was achieved, if there was any way to apply that within my own home, I would be beating down the door to find out how they did it! If there is anything from Lean that I could apply in my life, in my home, or even back at my work – I would implement it in a second . . . and believe it or not, I have done just that with great success.

You might be wondering, what are these Lean Principles? Well, in the next chapter I am going to go into detail into four Lean principles that will revolutionize your family. But for this chapter there are two things I hope you will get out of it.

First, there are business ideas, tools, or methods that we can apply to our lives outside of work that will help us. Second, the world is changed by solutions that come from ideas that were sparked by a single question to a problem. So, never stop questioning. Never stop looking for solutions. Because who knows, but you might be the next person who comes up with an idea that will change the world.

# CHAPTER 2

## Four Principles of Lean That Will Forever Change the Way You Think

*Incorporate these four Lean principles into your life and the resulting mindset shift will change the way you see the world and positively affect the way you parent.*

W hile there are numerous principles associated with Lean, I chose four specific principles to focus on for the purposes of this book. These four principles can be summed up by the following: *Empower people* to *improve value* and *eliminate waste* so you can achieve *continuous improvement*. If that sounds simple, it's because Lean *is* simple. These four main principles of Lean have the potential to change your life. If used correctly, they can help make you a better parent through Continuous Family Improvement™.

Before I dive into these principles, let me ask you a question to help illustrate what the philosophy of Lean is all about. Is the glass half full or half empty?

How do you see it? Don't worry about being judged as an optimist or a pessimist. How do you see it?

One of my sons tells my wife and I that while we are discussing this question, he says he'll drink the water in the glass because he's an opportunist. But how did you answer? Half full? Half empty?

Someone who is trained to think in Lean doesn't see it as either half full or half empty. They see that you are using the wrong sized glass or that there might be another issue with the glass or the water. They look at it and wonder, "What is the water to be used for?" "Is there a problem with the faucet that it was only able to fill it up half way?" "How often do you need the water?" "Who is the water for?" "Is the water purified?" "Is the water the right temperature?" "Is the glass in the right location?" And the questions go on and on.

Those with a Lean mindset will figure out how to fill up the glass for you quicker, in the right sized glass, in the right location, and at the ideal temperature for you. Then they will get it for you in the most efficient manner possible. Lean is a unique way of thinking. A different way to see the world.

Now that we've established that Lean has a unique take on life, let's look at the four principles I promised to discuss. Because these four principles are going to lay the foundation for Parenting the Lean Way.

### Principle 1: Valuing the Individual

The first principle of Lean that I want to discuss is that of *Valuing the Individual*. Personally, I wish that more companies did this. Those companies that apply this principle find that by empowering staff their production and innovation increase, their employee engagement and retention are at all-time highs, and their customers are better served by their employees. Valuing the Individual is all about empowering them to make better decisions, supporting them to learn new skills, and developing greater competency in their areas of responsibility. It's also about listening and acting upon the ideas for improvement that people have.

Just like businesses have room for improvement on this front, so do we as parents. There is a great quote attributed to Stacia Tauscher that sums this up perfectly, "We worry about what a child will be tomorrow, yet we forget that he is someone today."

There seems to be a growing trend in the world today, where parents are having a harder time letting go of their children. 'Helicopter Parent' is now a well-known term. When our children are young we must watch over them and protect them. It's natural. But as their children grow, some parents find it hard to adjust their parenting skills to let their children both make mistakes and learn from those mistakes. They prevent their children from having the autonomy of making their own decisions. They maintain control. They micromanage their kids. The dichotomy is that in the parent's efforts to protect and keep their children safe, they are hindering their growth and stunting their maturity. Their children are unprepared to face the world by themselves.

Don't forget to focus on who your child is today. Valuing the Individual is all about loving them for who they are now. It's about loving them enough to allow them to make their own decisions, and then supporting them or allowing them to face the consequences (good or bad) of their actions. Trial and error is a powerful learning tool that shows our children we value them, we trust them, and we love them for the individuals they are.

As parents, Valuing the Individual helps us see our children as something more than a child, but as an individual who will someday, sooner than we expect, become an adult. Valuing our children means that we trust them enough to give them more and more responsibilities. To let them make decisions. If you value the individual at home, their self-esteem will skyrocket. Their belief in themselves will grow as they see your belief in them grow.

We will discuss this principle in greater depth throughout this book, but this principle alone has the potential to transform your family relationships in ways you won't believe.

## Principle 2: Maximizing Value

The second principle of Lean is *Maximizing Value*. Now the business definition of value in this context is "Anything you do to a product or service that your customer is willing to pay for if they knew you were doing it." What does this definition mean for the family?

Keeping that definition in mind you need to ask yourself, "Is what I'm doing right now providing value that will make a difference in my family member's life either now or in the future?" The principle of maximizing value is not defined by you, but by others. To internalize this principle, you need a change in your mind frame. When you begin looking at your actions through the eyes of the person or persons you are serving, then you are beginning to embrace this Lean principle into your life.

Some call this servant leadership. But it's more than just that, it is thinking with purpose and with a long-term vision, so that when you interact with others, you are thinking about what will provide them with the best experience. Providing value takes thought and effort, but the returns are phenomenal, especially when we apply it to our parenting.

As a parent, when we try and maximize the value we provide, it can take on many forms. It could be about maximizing your money by making the dollar stretch further in your food or clothing budget. It could be about maximizing the emotional interactions you have with your family. It is also about providing them with our time. Being fully present with your spouse and children and practicing active listening skills, increases the value you provide to them. It could be about doing things that will provide positive lasting memories.

There is a great adage that has had a profound impact on my life and my parenting that says, "No amount of success can compensate for failure in the home." Maximizing value will cause you to question your own parenting to proactively reflect on your actions to see if your actions will add value to those you are serving. The next chapter will address this principle of Lean in greater depth.

## Principle 3: Eliminating Waste

The third principle of Lean is Eliminating Waste. If something is not providing value, then it is the opposite of value, or in Lean terms, what we call "waste."

Waste takes many forms in our life (which will be discussed in greater depth in Chapter 4), but so much of what we do has waste associated with it. An unkind word or action, a missed opportunity to really connect with our spouse or children, throwing away food, re-washing dishes because of food stuck to the plate (like egg yolks – my personal pet peeve), or even a red sock.

A red sock? How can that be waste? Well if you put it in with a white load of laundry, it can create a whole bunch of waste. Not only do you have pink clothes, but then you spend money to replace your ruined clothes.

Waste is all around us. You are probably wasting more money than you even realize. Did you know that the average American household of four is estimated to throw away between $1,350 – $2,275 per year in wasted food[iii]? If you could reduce that amount of waste by 50%, you would be saving close to a $1,000 per year. That's huge!

Reducing and eliminating waste is not only about improving systems, like doing the laundry, dishes, cooking, or maintaining a car, it is also about improving ourselves as an individual. While it's not always easy to take the time and self-analyze our own weaknesses and flaws, there are plenty of areas where we can all make improvements. Think of how much better your life would be if you took time to systematically eliminate those character flaws and weaknesses that hinder you from being your best.

How great would we be if as parents we could teach our children to examine themselves for those things that don't add value to their lives? Can you imagine your children following your example and actively working on their own, without your influence, to eliminate and strengthen their own weaknesses? Learning how to reduce the waste in our life is part of Parenting the Lean Way.

### Principle 4: Continuous Improvement

The final principle of Lean is ***Continuous Improvement***. If we are positively affecting the things we want to improve, then we will never be done, and that is the beauty of continuous improvement, or *Kaizen* as the Japanese call it.

Continuous improvement is often confused with perfection. It's not. When people fall short of an unrealistic desire to be perfect it can create feelings of guilt, inadequacy, hopelessness, and worthlessness. This in turn can lead to depression because they feel they will never measure up to the unrealistically high standards they set for themselves. You or your children should never confuse continuous improvement with perfection.

Continuous improvement is liberating and empowering. It welcomes failure as long as you learn from your mistakes, especially fast failures. A fast failure is made quickly at the start before you get too deep into trying to solve a problem so that you can adjust course and get back on track. Continuous improvement uplifts you with every incremental step forward. It reduces stress and creates harmony as you unlock your full potential with gradual steps. It sees life not as a race but as a journey.

Continuous improvement is a natural part of our lives, and yet the older we get, the less we practice it. Babies don't start out walking. First, they roll over and begin building their muscles. Then they start to crawl. Next, they begin to stand, to gain their balance, and of course they fall down, but they get back up. This is quickly followed by taking a few steps as they hold onto something. As their confidence grows, they take their first step unassisted. They promptly fall over. They try again, and down they go. The miracle is, they don't quit. They know it can be done, because they see us do it. They continuously try until they can do it too. And the next thing we know, they're running.

Before 1954, it was considered an impossibility for man to run a four-minute mile. Roger Bannister continuously improved until he broke the four-minute barrier. Within the decade, dozens of men had also broken that barrier, including a high school student. Now it's a common occurrence. In fact, in my high school there were twin brothers who could easily run the four-minute mile. It is only possible through continuous improvement.

If there is something in your life, in your family, or in your parenting you want to fix – continuous improvement will help you achieve your dreams.

One thing I have noticed as a business consultant and having lived in Japan, is that there is a fundamental difference between the Japanese mind frame when it comes to their view of continuous improvement (*Kaizen*) versus the Western perception. Typically, in business, as individuals in Western cultures are taught about continuous improvement, they focus on improving the problem, achieving their goals, calling it done and a success, and then promptly forgetting about the word 'continuous' in continuous improvement, because the problem has been remediated.

The Japanese, on the other hand, first used continuous improvement to save days and hours off their processes. Then they worked on shaving off minutes, later seconds, and now fifty years later they are still working on continuous improvement on the same processes by trying to figure out how to get tenths of a second off their process time. When I say continuous improvement, I mean continuous in every sense of the word.

\* \* \*

In the previous chapter, I mention two words over and over that are essential components of continuous improvement: effectiveness and efficiency. In business, and I believe in life, these two words are very important concepts. They are concepts that unfortunately often confuse people.

Here is an easy way to remember them: being effective is about doing the right things, while being efficient is about doing things right. Be careful here because Peter Drucker, the father of management, warned, "There is nothing so useless as doing efficiently, that which should not be done at all."

These two concepts can make your life easier, but they must be used together. First, be effective in what you do by prioritizing the things you need to do. Second, when you do something, do it right the first time, with quality, and in a timely manner; that's being efficient.

Teaching our children these concepts will have an immeasurable benefit in their lives – truly a gift worth giving. This book is all about helping you as a parent to show your family how to embrace Continuous Family Improvement™ in your home. While these concepts are based from a business context, we want to use these Lean tools in a way that is best situated for an individual and personal context. This means adapting these tools and concepts to demonstrate the love and concern we have for our children.

Remember to ask questions. Because as we learned in the last chapter, questions have the power to change the world. When we are on autopilot through life and we don't question things, we can't make improvements to ourselves or our environment. Always question things to gain a deeper understanding. Think convenience, think efficiency, think of ways to increase value and eliminate waste. There is always a more effective and efficient way to do something. Look for it. Find it. Make it happen. And above all, live in the moment and value and love those around you.

There you have it, the four principles of Lean that we will focus on in the chapters ahead: Valuing the Individual, Maximizing Value, Eliminating Waste, and Continuous Improvement.

Has your perception of the question, "Is the glass half-full or half-empty" changed? I hope these principles of Lean have at least started you thinking that there might be something more than just two answers to that question. The mind set shift that occurs when you embrace these Lean principles will naturally cause you to look at the glass differently, or in the case of this book, look at parenting differently.

The Lean Way will help you to also see relationships and interactions in a new light as well. Just like none of our children are the same, there is not one way to parent. We need to be flexible and agile in how we parent. We need to be able to quickly adjust our parenting techniques and customize our approach to best help each child based on their individual needs. Parenting the Lean Way is about having that agility to focus and adapt our parenting quickly to meet the needs of each child and the family as a whole, with all the love and concern we can give them.

# CHAPTER 3

## Increase Focus by Adding Value – A Twist on the Golden Rule

*In business value is seen from the viewpoint of the customer. At home, how often do we think about or understand what the other person really values?*

There's a story of a man who saw three bricklayers working. Curious, he asked the first, "What are you doing?" The man looked at his watch and said curtly, "I'm laying bricks until I can get out of here at five." Still not knowing what they were building, he asked the second one, "What are you doing?" The man continued working and told him he was simply building a wall. Still wanting to know what they were building, he came up to the third brick layer who was humming while intently concentrating on his work, "What are you doing?" The brick layer, who was engrossed in his work, finished laying the brick he was working on, turned to the man, and with a smile on his face and an exuberance in his voice, looked up into the sky and said, "Son, I'm building a cathedral to my God and a place of worship for my neighbors."

These three men each had a different perspective of the value they were contributing. One did the bare minimum – just enough to collect his paycheck. Another knew the task he was assigned, and though he didn't see the bigger picture, was competently completing the task of building a wall. Only one knew the purpose and had the proper perspective. Only one was putting in his whole soul into his work. He knew who his customers were, those he was serving, and more importantly – what they wanted. This third bricklayer was working from a position of empowerment. He didn't need to be told what to do. He wasn't going to cut corners. In fact, it was because of his devotion that he put additional effort into his craftsmanship to create added value.

It's amazing what a difference your attitude can make on the work you do. A poor attitude and the day can go on forever. A positive, engaged attitude helps the day fly by.

As parents, we need to employ this business concept of Maximizing Value into our lives. Creating value is as much a business tool as it is a philosophy of life.

What does this mean? It means that instead of just going through the motions of being a parent, a spouse, a sibling, a friend, a colleague or a boss, we should actively be thinking of what value we are adding to those we associate with. We should seek to understand from their perspective what they want from us.

This concept has the power to save marriages from divorce, transform rebellious teenagers, resolve sibling disputes, and improve the love and relationships in your family.

Value ultimately is not in how we define it; it is in how those we serve define it. This concept I'm talking about is the next step in the Golden Rule. No longer can you be satisfied with serving others by: "Doing unto others as you would have them do unto you." We need to move to a higher level, "Do unto others as *they* would like done unto *themselves.*" It's a subtle difference, but one that makes a tremendous impact on those we love.

Focusing on providing value to others moves the focus away from ourselves. We need to stretch our capacity to create value in the lives of others. We need to provide more value than is expected. A long-term perspective is essential. When we help others, we need to make them feel like they are the most important person in our life.

How do we do that? Well, one way is to have a paradigm shift. World renowned author and businessman Stephen R. Covey talks about this idea in his book The Seven Habits of Highly Effective People. He tells of a time when riding on the train he found that he was irritated with a man who couldn't control his children, as they were running around bothering the other passengers. Stephen turned to this father and politely called his attention to it.

The man apologized and told him that they were returning home from the hospital where his wife had just died and that both he and his children didn't quite know how to deal with the loss. Instantly, Stephen's paradigm shifted and the feeling of irritation he had seconds earlier towards this father, who couldn't or wouldn't control his kids, was gone.

Empathy had replaced irritation. He wanted to help. As Covey put it, "Suddenly I *saw* things differently, and because I *saw* differently, I *thought* differently, I *felt* differently, I *behaved* differently.[iv]"

The fact is, as parents, as people, we only know a small portion of what is really going on in any given situation. We know mostly what is happening with our thoughts, emotions, and experiences. We might correctly interpret some of the superficial actions of what we see in others. Generally, we make an educated guess when reading situations. *But* this is only our perspective of reality.

We cannot know the thoughts, feelings, and experiences of others. We don't know what issues they are working on – and if we did, our paradigm, the way we see the situation, might change completely. This, in turn, can change our behavior, our feelings, and our relationships.

We also tend to make allowances for strangers more than those closest to us. If we have someone over for dinner and they spill a glass, or break it, we are polite, and don't make a big deal about it. If our child does it, we might not be as forgiving.

Have you ever been in a situation where you are irritated or having a fight with a family member and then the phone rings? When you answer it, you instantly change your tone of voice, you smile, and the person on the other end would never have been able to tell what your state had been just seconds before.

Now, if we can change our paradigms in an instant, or our tone of voice to answer a phone, or be forgiving to a stranger, then we can do that for our family.

We need to be able to create value for others. When we are concentrating on helping others, we spend less time thinking about ourselves and our problems, and more time adding value. This helps us feel more fulfilled. This is one of the secrets to happiness.

A little caveat here, sometimes the realization of that value doesn't come instantly. Instead, it comes sometime in the future, especially for kids. When adding value, think in terms of both what adds value now, as well as what will add value in the long term.

Remember, creating value, is always from the perspective of the other person.

One mind set change we can all benefit from is increasing the length of time we plan for things. Sure, we could do things for our kids, but long term that is robbing them of the ability and the know-how to do things for themselves. They may not appreciate it when we ask them to do their chores, but as they form the habits of picking up after themselves and keeping their home clean, in time they will come to see the value of the work ethic that you gave to them. Their future families will likewise appreciate the value you provided your children. So, don't be afraid to focus on the long-term value, as well as the short-term value.

Let me share with you a personal story that will help illustrate how taking the long-term view on adding value can improve the way that you do things. Five years ago, my first daughter was born. As I was holding her, I thought about what my life would be like with my daughter. My thoughts came to that day in the future when she would get married and the traditional father-daughter dance. How wonderful that day would be. Then there was a terrifying thought, what if something happened and I couldn't be there? I wondered how could I add value to my daughter on her wedding day, regardless if I was there or not?

That got me thinking. Then the thought hit me, and an innovative idea occurred to me because of the questions I had asked about how to create value. Every year on her birthday, I would dress up in my tuxedo, I would buy her a white dress, and I would share a birthday dance with my daughter. I would make it a tradition. Every year I get out the video camera and we have our dance.

On her wedding day, before our dance if I'm there, or in place of it if I'm not, we will play a compilation of all our dances. Every time we turn, it will fade into the next year's dance, so that you will see her age one year at a time. I believe that this will make her special day even more special, something that will add value for her on her wedding day.

Do you see the impact that can happen to your life and the lives of others? All because you put some thought into how you can provide value for those around you.

This is may be a simple example, but this is part of what it means to be a parent the Lean Way. Short-term, long-term, your thoughts begin to change as you contemplate how to put that cherry on top of your interactions.

When you embrace this principle of adding value, magic begins to happen in your home. When you actively look for ways to add value in your home, it will help increase the love you feel for each other.

In this chapter, I hope you realize that by seeing the larger picture of what we are doing, the value we create can bless the lives of others, as well as increase our happiness. A key tool of becoming Lean in business is creating value for the customer. By sacrificing a little of what we want, we receive far more than we give up. You create memories that your family will treasure forever. Your relationships deepen, communication increases, and you are proactive in your parenting.

Our focus should always be on increasing the value we add to others, especially our family members. This might seem to be a simple tool, but it requires discipline and effort to retrain your thoughts to constantly be on the lookout for opportunities to serve and to add value. The effort will be worth it.

This is the first step to transforming your home life for the better. By taking the time to think about it from the other's point of view, we can increase the love and harmony in our homes, and eliminate the contention and argumentativeness that might exist.

*"Strive not to be a success,*
*but rather to be of value."*

*- Albert Einstein*

*"If parents pass enthusiasm along to their children,*
*they will leave them an estate of incalculable value."*

*- Thomas Edison*

*"If there is any one secret of success,
it lies in the ability to get the other person's point of view
and see things from that person's angle
as well as from your own."*

*- Henry Ford*

# CHAPTER 4

## To Improve Our Lives,
## We Need to Identify and Remove Waste

*A fundamental concept of Lean is that there is waste in everything. Our job is to find it, and then reduce or eliminate that waste.*

In Lean methodology, if you were to place value on one side of a coin, then waste would have to go on the other. These two concepts are pretty equally balanced in terms of importance. They are nearly opposite sides of the same coin. Together they make continuous improvement possible. Understanding what waste is will help your family recognize it when they see it and then take steps to eliminate it. You must be able to both increase the value of an activity and remove or reduce any waste associated with it to achieve true improvement.

Let's examine what waste is from a business perspective, what waste might look like in a family situation, and why it is important to reduce its impact in your life. When you learn to recognize waste, it will quite literally change the way you see the world. Ultimately, learning to see and eliminate waste and add value, will lead you to a state of continuous improvement – this is Lean.

How wonderful would it be for your family if you could stop the nagging and bickering, remove the clutter from your life (both the physical messiness and the emotional clutter from the baggage of your past), and reduce time wasters that prevent you from achieving your goals, while at the same time, improving the efficiency of your systems?

This is what Continuous Family Improvement™ is all about. Keep doing what works, stop doing what doesn't, and look for ways to get a little better every day.

When you adopt this mindset, the little improvements you make day by day help make your family life exceptional. Once you have learned to recognize waste, teach your children the concepts of value and waste and then empower them to do something about it.

There's a quote I like, "A man who dares to waste one hour of time has not discovered the value of life.v" I think the reason this quote resonates so much is because it goes along with something I teach in my workshops, "Our time is the only real currency we have to spend with our children.vi"

By understanding areas of your life that are wasteful, you can identify them, and then work at eliminating them. This will increase the time you have available, so you can spend it with your family doing the things that really matter to them.

Taiichi Ohno, considered the father of the Toyota Production System, originally categorized seven wastes. He created the seven wastes as a starting point, but said, "Waste is not limited to seven types, so don't bother thinking about 'what type of waste is this?' Just get on with it and do Kaizenvii." (Kaizen is the Japanese word for continuous improvement).

A manufacturing industry standard acronym uses eight categories of waste in the form of DOWNTIME to make it easier to remember. These waste categories are:

*De*fects

*O*verproduction

*W*aiting

*N*ot Fully Utilizing People

*Tr*ansportation

*In*ventory

*M*otion

*Ex*cess Processing

I'll give some examples in a moment of each of these wastes as they relate to the home, but there is another category that was left out of the business definition of waste that I feel should be included in a family context. This is the waste of *Negative Emotions*. It is that side of human interactions that include things like anger, attitude, frustration, revenge, miscommunications, assumptions, a martyrdom mentality or a defeatist mentality, incorrect or debilitating beliefs, and the list could go on and on.

These are the emotions and perspectives that when acted upon, damage our relationships with our family members and others. The harm that can result is clearly waste. I'm not saying you shouldn't have or feel these emotions, it is part of what make us human. We should however minimize their negative impacts, especially on our family.

Inherently, I think we know waste when we see it, but some elements of waste are subtle, and often overlooked. I want you to see how many of these resonate with you.

**Defects** in manufacturing are discarded. All the time, energy, and materials that went into a defective product are wasted, and you must still rework it. Worst yet is if it slips past quality control and makes it into the hands of the customer. Because then you also have a dissatisfied customer who may never come back. So, what does this look like in the home?

I previously mentioned the example of the red sock in the load of white clothes and how it produces a defective pink load of laundry. In all fairness, I only did that once and I was only 16. I haven't done that since, thankfully. Defects are a major form of waste because they cause you to rework, redo, or worse, re-purchase something. What a waste of time and money because something wasn't done right the first time.

**Overproduction** or **Overprocessing** is simply producing more than is required or requested. According to the Natural Resources Defense Council "the average U.S. household of four produces in food waste between $1,350 to $2,275 in annual losses.[viii]" Part of this waste is from making more than we can consume before it spoils, and we throw it out. If you can reduce this waste in your home by roughly 1%, you've not only paid for this book, but you have more disposable money than when you started. Not bad for a one percent improvement.

In addition to food overproduction, here is an example of overproduction from the business world that might be affecting your health today. The average size of the U.S. dinner plate is 36% bigger now than it was in 1960[ix], and arguably Americans are also 36% larger today than in 1960. I say this only partly in jest, but dinner plates going from 9 inches to 12 inches does seem to be a bit of overproduction, especially when coupled with the unhealthy belief we were all taught as kids to "clean our plates" – thus we need larger belts.

**Waiting**, what better example of waste is there than waiting? How much time do we spend waiting? Research shows that the average person spends five years waiting in lines, eight months opening junk mail, six months waiting at traffic lights, and one year looking for lost possessions during their lifetime[x]. What would you do with all that extra time if you could eliminate just some of that wasted time waiting? Or use that time for more productive value-added activities?

***Not Fully Utilizing People*** is one of the most tragic of all wastes. Unused human potential, whether at work or at home, is completely avoidable. Do you allow your children the opportunity to creatively think of ways to add value to the family or solve their own problems? Do you encourage them to pursue their talents and interests, or do you unintentionally stifle their love of learning or creativity by being a helicopter parent, swooping in and rescuing them when they are perfectly capable of doing things for themselves? None of us are perfect, and we have all been guilty of this in one form or another, but realizing that this is a waste allows us to figure out ways to eliminate it out of our words, actions, and thoughts.

By becoming Lean, we look for ways to add value for our family members. One of those ways is by empowering those around us to do more. There is magic that happens when we eliminate the waste of not fully utilizing people, but instead trust those we love to contribute more value and to be more responsible in the home.

***Transportation*** is a common waste. Have you ever driven to the store, gone shopping, and returned home only to realize that the one thing you needed to get, you forgot? Have you ever driven back to the store to get that item? If you have, then you understand the waste of transportation.

***Inventory*** as a waste takes two forms: The first is stuff. This is the inventory of extra items you don't need now or might never use. The second is space. This is the space the inventory takes up that you could be using for other things.

Let's say, for example, that you have a room you fill with all the things you mean to put away. You know the room – the one you don't want guests to see. In the U.S., the average home size is just over 2,400 sq.ft. and the average monthly mortgage is nearly $1,700; this means that for an 8' x 10' room you are paying $1,400 per year for the privilege of paying a storage fee for all that stuff in a room you can't use or enjoy. Is that stuff even worth that amount? Talk about waste.

The waste of **Motion** is defined as the energy spent in excessive, strenuous, and/or unnecessary motions. This is different from the waste of transportation where the focus is on travel and distance. Motion is about unnecessary repetitive movements. Scrubbing dishes hours after the food has dried, instead of simply rinsing the plates when finished, is an example of the waste of motion. It could also be trying to lift something too heavy, or needing to move your foot ladder every time you get something out of a cupboard.

The waste of **Excess Processing** is defined as the excessive generation of materials or information beyond the customer's needs. If your child asks for scrambled eggs without pepper and you add pepper, you didn't provide the customer (your child) with what they wanted. The effort you took to get the pepper, shake it on the eggs, and put the pepper away was all wasted energy that did not need to take place. Plus, the customer (your child) is likely to reject the food, thus leading to more waste in both the food and the time for needing to prepare something else.

I'm not talking about not giving your kids vegetables because they don't want them. They might see this as value, but it would clearly be waste. Providing proper nutrition is extremely important, and as parents we have the knowledge and experience to know the difference. Rather, something inconsequential like not putting pepper on the eggs is an example of excess processing waste.

*Negative Emotions* is the final type of waste. Does it do any good for yourself or your family when you feel frustrated, angry, resentful or any one of a hundred other emotional states that increase your stress, deprive you of your happiness, leave you feeling drained, or cause contention in your home? I'm not suggesting you should never experience these emotions, or that we become logical unemotional beings, far from it.

What I am suggesting is that everyone has the ability to control their emotional state, and with personal discipline, we can make an effort to reduce those emotions that cause harm. Some of these emotions at the proper time are therapeutic, and at other times cause damage. I'm advocating for a little emotional intelligence to tell the difference.

Think about it, if you had a tough day at work or school and come home and yell at a family member because you were frustrated – and not because of anything they did – you wasted time in an action that did not add value to the situation. You were responsible for a reaction that if you had given thought to it beforehand, you could have avoided being short with your loved one. Instead you damaged the relationship you had with that family member.

Time is then wasted feeling regret for the inappropriate way you acted. Regret, if focused on and not moved passed, can be a huge waste because it leaves you stuck in the past instead of present in the now and looking forward to the future. Life really is too short to fill it with regret or any other negative emotion that doesn't add value to ourselves or others.

Finally, you need to spend additional time trying to repair the damage you did by yelling in the first place. By being aware of our emotional state, we can gain control over how we are feeling, what we say, and we avoid the emotional waste that comes from letting our emotions run us, instead of us running our emotions.

Do you believe that last statement? If you don't, I'm here to tell you that it's true. It may not be easy, but each of us can control our own emotions. It takes effort. It takes being aware of your own emotional state in the first place, but isn't it worth the effort?

This is the only category of waste that only you can control. You can't do it for others, and they can't do it for you. To control your own emotions or to avoid pushing the buttons of others, accomplishes both the elimination of waste and the adding of value. I believe that our families are worth that effort.

No one at the end of their life says, "I wish I had spent more time at the office." Rather they remember good memories [*value*] (the family vacations, the time you spent working together in the garden), *and* unfortunately, they also remember the bad memories [*waste*] (the unkind words, the fights, and every time you were perceived as unfair).

Some dear friends of mine once took care of an aging aunt. In the twilight of her life she was facing dementia, yet she could recall with perfect retention every sharp, hurtful, and unkind word her father had used to demean her when she was younger. This story acts as a warning for each of us. I want to be the example for my children that they will want to follow. I don't want them to remember me for being overly critical and condescending. Rather, I want my children to remember me for encouraging, supporting, and empowering them.

Sometimes, our encouragement can sound like criticism to our children. Remember, it doesn't matter how we intended it; what matters is how they perceived it. We need to learn how to present our messages of encouragement in a way that adds value to them and is not seen as waste. We therefore need to be close to our children and understand how they are feeling about things. We need to be willing to adjust our behavior for their sakes.

As parents, we should be even more considerate and thoughtful toward our children. These aren't strangers that we are forced to be around at work. These are the most precious individuals in the world to us. We need to treat them accordingly. We need to be willing to put the work in to have strong relationships so that our family knows just how much we love them. That happens when we learn to recognize the emotional waste we generate, and we work to reduce or eliminate it out of our lives.

Here is something else as parents we need to remember, if there is something in the behavior of our children that we do not like, something that we see as waste, our children are in more ways than we like to admit, mirror reflections of us. We might be providing them with the example of the waste, that in turn is bothering us. Changing our children starts with changing ourselves.

When we change our attitude what can happen? Have you ever been around someone who had a great attitude, even when doing a task that might not have been the most pleasant? Working with that person can make the task not seem so hard, difficult, or boring. Time flies when you are working around someone like that. A positive attitude can add value. As parents, we need to be like that.

Conversely, working around someone that complains about everything, can not only make the same task unbearable, but also time seems to drag on and on, and on... because it does. It actually takes longer to do something when working with a negative attitude, which is waste.

One of our kids once complained for over an hour about how unfair it was that he had to put something away in the dishwasher.

In the end, he did it in about 30 seconds, a 120:1 ratio of waste to value. Definitely there was some room for improvement!

* * *

Now that you can recognize what waste is, you can begin to work on ways to eliminate it from your life. As a family, you can make a game out of finding areas that create waste and try to eliminate that waste and replace it by adding value.

For example, as a family we put our shoes in the closet by our front door when we enter the house. I wasted so much time looking in that dark closet for my shoes. "What waste," I thought. "Why do I complain about it every day? Do something about it."

On the way home from work that night, I bought automatic motion sensor LED lights and installed them in the closet. Now when I open the door, the light comes on and I can see the shoes. This is obviously one very simple example, but *Kazoku Kaizen*, or Continuous Family Improvement™, is all about finding trivial things like this and improving it.

Thus, little by little these improvements will add up value to greatly reduce the daily stress at home and make our lives easier. You will gain back time and improve your relationships. Reallocate the currency of your life, time, back into your family with value-added activities that will make memories. That is truly the best investment any of us will ever make, and what makes Parenting the Lean Way different.

I have a challenge for you. With your family's help, identify waste, then work together to find ways to reduce or eliminate it from your family life. Prioritize your list, and one by one start working on making your life simpler. As you do, there will be fewer and fewer things to complain about, and your life will get easier and easier with less worry and stress.

Waste is all around us, and one of the biggest wastes within a family tends to be a lack of communication. This is more than an issue of the generation gap between parents and children, it's about not taking the time to give adequate attention to the process of communication. In the next chapter, I will introduce you to a tool that is going to help eliminate some of the waste that happens from miscommunication. This tool alone will transform your family in ways that you can't even begin to imagine.

# CHAPTER 5

## The Family Board is a Powerful Visual Management Tool

*The Family Board is the first tool you will use. It will become your family's communication center. All your improvement efforts will be made transparent and visual through the Family Board.*

There is a saying that a picture is worth a thousand words. This is true. We are visual beings. We read pictures and graphs faster than words and numbers. Visual management improves company performance, and it can do the same at home. Peter Drucker said, "You can't manage what you can't measure." And he said, "If you can't measure it, you can't improve it." Visual management is a strong element of Lean, because it makes things easier to internalize. It will help make your life easier at home.

### The Power of Visual Management

Here's a great example of visual management from the business world. I can go anywhere in the world into any well-run manufacturing floor – it doesn't matter what the industry is – and I can tell you instantly if they are ahead of schedule, on schedule, or behind schedule. If there is a problem anywhere in the plant, I can tell you instantly what machine is having the issue. At a team station, I can tell you who is doing what job, what their skill levels are with any given task, and how long it has been since the last accident. I can tell you what parts are running low in inventory. What's really cool is that I can tell you how to do any task in that manufacturing plant, even though I have never done that job before.

How can I tell you so much? Visual management is the key. Everything I just mentioned is detailed out in visual management charts, graphs, sign boards, status boards, standard work instructions and a host of other visual management tools. These same visual management tools are used in manufacturing, offices, hospitals, banks, and even in fast food restaurants, to improve their efficiency.

To grasp the impact of visual management for yourself, check out this fabulous ad from Land Rover to see the power found in a Silhouette Board – another visual management tool. At a glance, you can tell exactly what is missing from the Silhouette Board. Compare that to the detailed list below of the same items. It takes an incredible amount of time longer for you to both read and comprehend it, when compared to the instant recognition that comes from the Silhouette Board. That's the power of visual management.

**THE POWER OF VISUAL MANAGEMENT:** Which is easier to see what was taken? This ad from Land Rover or the List of Tools? This is a perfect example of the power of visual management.

As parents, we can use the power of visual management to make our home life simpler. Have you ever asked your child, or spouse, if they have done something, only to have them get upset with you because they have already done it and they felt your casual reminder was an accusation? With a visual management system in your home, you wouldn't need to ask, you can see instantly what they have done, and what is left to do. You can see where the problems

(Copy of advertisement (top) provided by Jaguar Land Rover North America, LLC.)

are. You can see how everyone is progressing with their goals, projects, or anything else they are working on. How is this done? The Family Board is the crown jewel of Parenting the Lean Way and is based on the Lean business tool of the Kanban board.

### The Kanban Board

In business, it goes by many names: team board, progress board, scrum board, production board, and the list could go on. Regardless of what you call it, it is essentially a Kanban Board. What is a Kanban Board? Kanban is Japanese for signboard or billboard.

In the IT side of business with Agile, they have refined the Kanban Board into a project management tool, a time management tool, and a visual management tool that helps the team to work together to complete their jobs for the customer. It helps them to figure out how to add extra value to their work.

The Kanban Board is versatile, it can be done anywhere. Typically, whiteboards are used, but they can be done on a bulletin board, a chalkboard, a wall, a door, a window, a desk, a piece of paper, in a book or planner, or online. A Kanban Board can be used anywhere. Sticky notes are often the preferred method for writing down tasks, because it's easy to move them around the board.

I have used a Kanban Board at work for organizational change management initiatives, team projects, coordinating departments, for my work and personal tasks, and I even use it at home. Everywhere I've used it, people have loved it.

As a consultant, the managers and executives I have worked with love it because they know exactly what everyone is working on and if there are any problems, they can tell instantly what those are. They can look at the board and know the status of what's been done without anyone being there to explain it to them. This saves time, answers questions, and makes their job and mine easier.

The magic of the Kanban Board is that it improves communication by providing a change in perspective. In most businesses directions, orders, and decisions are made at the top and communicated down the hierarchical chain. This is known as a typical top-down communication or leadership style.

The Kanban Board changes this traditional top-down style because it empowers everyone to share what they are working on, make decisions and recommendations, and communicate successes and risks upwards to top management. This is a bottom-up communication or leadership style. It is a powerful tool in business.

The Kanban Board will be able to help your family too — plus it's easy to use. The basic Kanban Board has four elements to it.

First, the task cards: put all the tasks you need to complete on individual sticky notes or cards. In the simplest form, you just write down the task to be done. Many people find that you get more out of a task if you explain what the task is, why it is important (the value you're adding), who is responsible for completing the task, and when it needs to be completed. Do what works best for you and your family.

The next three elements of the Kanban Board are for tracking the tasks. They are divided into: To Do, Doing, and Done.

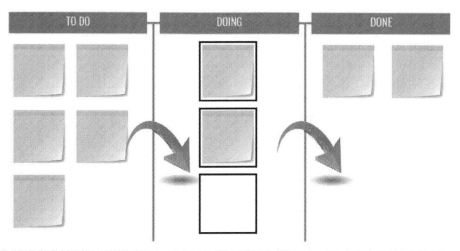

DON'T FORGET TO LIMIT YOUR WORK IN PROGRESS (WIP) TO NO MORE THAN THREE

Put all your tasks into your "To Do" column. The Kanban Board will help you prioritize tasks better. When the tasks are visible it is easier to organize, prioritize, and move them around. By seeing all your tasks in one place and knowing which tasks are your highest priority, you are able to get more done.

Next, choose your most important task you need to complete and move it over into the "Doing" column. A key thing to remember with the "Doing" column is that you will want to limit your Work in Progress (WIP). I recommend no more than three tasks in this column at any given time. Ideally only one or two tasks.

You might be wondering why you don't put all your tasks into the doing column. You've got to get them all done anyway, so why limit the tasks you are working on? You might even think that you are great at multi-tasking.

The idea that multi-tasking makes you more efficient is a myth. In fact, research[xi] has shown you get less done when you are trying to multitask multiple items than when you concentrate on one item at a time. Not only is it easier to concentrate on only one task at a time, but you can complete the tasks faster when you are not wasting time switching back and forth between activities.

Finally, as you complete a task, move it into the "Done" column and then select another task from the "To Do" column and move it to the "Doing" column, and repeat the process until you have completed everything you needed to. There is a little bit more to it than that, but this gives you a general idea about how to use a Kanban Board.

There is significant satisfaction that comes from completing a task, and the Kanban Board makes that process visual. That visual element also positions you to be able to see everything you need to get accomplished in one place, which in turn will help you to prioritize your most important tasks first.

## The Family Board

The Family Board is a much more in-depth tool than a simple Kanban Board, but it's not complicated. The Family Board is adaptable to fit your family's needs. There are just a few more elements than the Kanban Board's "To Do," "Doing," and "Done." The Family Board Meeting is the engine that runs Parenting the Lean Way. It will help coordinate all the phases of the GATES™ system (explained in the next chapter).

There are numerous additional elements that you can add beyond a simple Kanban section to give your Family Board a personality and life that will fit the needs of your family. I recommend having five sections:

**1.** A Kanban Section. This section helps drive your schedules, tasks, and household chores.

**2.** Your Family Values. I will show you how to create your family values in Chapter 8.

**3.** A Recognition Section. This is a place to recognize and encourage positive behaviors.

**4.** An Opportunity Section. Family members identify opportunities to solve problems.

**5.** A Goal Section. Track your momentum in reaching your goals (Chapter 16 covers this).

Including these five sections in a Family Board has had the most influential impact on families who use the boards. Please note, this is not an exhaustive list of what can be included. In our home, we have a thought of the day, which can include a quote, scripture, poem, or thought. We also have a prayer request section, which we update with people and things to remember in our prayers (I like this because it teaches the kids to think beyond their own needs and wants and focus on others).

Some families add sections for more specific things: homework, chores, projects, savings reached for vacations or the children's personal accounts, top five weekly goals, health and fitness schedule or goals, and a happiness meter to let everyone know how you are feeling. Whatever you decide to use, know that there is not a "right" or "wrong" way to make your Family Board. What matters is that you use the board by holding your Family Meetings regularly.

### Family Meetings

The Family Meeting along with the Family Board is going to transform the way your family communicates with each other. While it might be difficult at first, if you continue holding your Family Meetings, you will find your family relationships improving, and an increased sense of peace and organization in your home.

Ideally, the Family Meeting is a short ten to fifteen-minute meeting that you hold every day. Initially the parents will lead the meeting, ideally at the same time every day. I encourage everyone to gather at your Family Board and stand up, not sit down. If everyone is standing, it helps the meeting go quicker.

As the children become more familiar with how to run the board meeting, I recommend giving the children the opportunity to lead the meeting. This helps to boost confidence and build leadership skills in your kids. Our four-year-old will often lead our family meeting, and she does an excellent job.

The format of the Family Board Meeting is simple. Prior to the start of the meeting, everyone should gather at the board and update the status of their tasks, goals, and add any opportunities for improvement that they see, and recognitions that they want to give.

The meeting starts on time. It is important that everyone participates. If I'm out of town with work, I'll call in to participate over the phone. I encourage you to stress the importance of everyone participating and then have the commitment to follow through.

The person conducting welcomes everyone and starts off by covering any items that will be happening that day. This first part of the meeting is the Kanban section of the board. It could be assigning family chores, or discussing the logistics of transportation for the day. Referring to their tasks that they have on the board, everyone in turn will answer the following three questions. "What did you get accomplished yesterday?"; "What do you hope to get accomplished today?"; "Are there any roadblocks that are preventing you from achieving what you need to?" (i.e. Do you need any help?) That's it – very basic.

After everyone has had a turn sharing their day and plan, I like to take a moment to read any recognitions that may have been given. On our Family Board, we have what I refer to as "the Santa List." This is the "nice list", not the "naughty list". It is a space where any family member can acknowledge anyone else for something they did. We want the recognitions to be sincere, so we don't give recognitions to make each other feel good with false platitudes. What we do recognize are "right" behaviors and honest effort. When we give these recognitions, it reinforces to everyone that we noticed and appreciated what they did for the family. This part of our Family Board has done more to positively impact family behaviors than anything else.

For example, our eldest son once helped his younger brother with his homework, something he had never done, so we recognized him for doing that. Because we made a big deal about that at our Family Board Meeting, he felt good, his brother thanked him, and he was on top of the world. We noticed afterwards that he started going out of his way to see if his younger brother needed any help. This might not have happened if we hadn't shown appreciation. We highlighted the behavior we wanted to see, and he responded by doing more of it.

All of us have a natural tendency to focus on those things that we don't want. We criticize bad behaviors more than we compliment good ones. Unfortunately, that is part of human nature. The wonderful thing is, as humans, we can change our natural behaviors. Part of Parenting the Lean Way is to change your focus to highlight value. Focus on the good and the waste will be removed.

There is an illustration I like to use of two children climbing a tree. When the two different parents notice their children, each parent shouts a different message to their child. "Don't fall!" shouts one. The other calls up, "Hold on tight!" Would you care to guess which child fell? Inadvertently, the first parent while trying to be helpful, focused the child on the possibility of falling. While the other parent's message was centered on holding tight to the tree. Each word of caution created a different focus.

As parents, we have the power to shape our child's focus. Which way do you want your child to focus, on the negative or the positive? As parents, we must teach our children to focus on the good and beauty this world has to offer, this perspective will bless their childhood. This is the power of the recognition part of the Family Board – it forces you to look for positive things to focus on. This will transform your family. Communication will improve, concern and empathy will grow, and harmony in the family will increase.

My wife and I regularly recognize our kids when they do something good. And from time to time we also reinforce the transformations they have already made by recognizing them for the wonderful changes and effort they have made. They feel good and continue to do whatever the recognition was for.

Likewise, as parents we benefit because the children start using this as well to let us know what things they appreciated from us. We learn what they value, and it helps us be better parents. This particular part of the Family Board will change your life. I even record all the recognitions so that at the end of the year we can show the kids how much they accomplished – talk about a confidence booster.

The person leading the meeting will then review the family goals or KPIs (see Chapter 16) and have a brief discussion about how they can best achieve the goals the family is working on. This element of the Family Board will help you and your family to be accountable to each other for achieving your goals. By using this daily visual reminder of what you are trying to achieve, I can promise you that you will get more goals accomplished in a year than you thought possible.

Finally, you see if anyone has noticed any opportunities for improvement that need to be addressed. I like to refer to this section as opportunities for improvement, rather than problems. Phrasing it this way makes it seem easier to solve an opportunity for improvement than a problem. Again, it goes back to what you choose to focus on. This section helps you change your focus from the problem to the opportunity. From the consequences to the solution.

The interesting thing about the opportunity section is that you don't try to solve the opportunity in the Family Meeting. If you can solve it in under a minute, and you won't run over your fifteen minutes, then it might be appropriate to offer a solution.

If there is an opportunity for improvement (a "problem"), write it down. Share it in such a way as to not attack any family member. Refer to the behavior not the individual, or talk about the issue, ideally from the standpoint of the solution. Assign an owner for developing or carrying out the solution, and a time for them to share their plan or progress with the family, but that's it. Don't discuss the how-to's at the board. Remember, you only have fifteen minutes.

If you feel you must discuss something further, then just before ending the meeting ask the family member to come see you some time after the Family Board Meeting is over. This could be fifteen minutes after the meeting to several hours. Never discipline or offer correction during the Family Meeting.

Have a break before disciplining a child or helping them to solve a problem. If you do this, your children will love the Family Board Meetings because they know that it is a safe place to discuss what they are doing, and they will be willing to ask for help when they need it. Plus, the time break allows you to have time to think, to cool down if needed, and to be proactive in how to handle the situation.

And that's it. The Family Board Meeting is quite simple.

Some concluding thoughts about the Family Board Meetings: Keep it short. Don't go longer than 15 minutes. If you keep it short, the family will participate. They will love it because it is a time when they know that everyone is listening to them. Your Family Board Meeting is a time to focus on the positive. Solutions over problems. Right behaviors over wrong. It's about helping, listening, and creating structure and organization for your family.

A great way to do this is to set some basic family rules for your Family Board Meeting. Only one person speaks at a time. You must treat the meeting as a safe place. This means that you never criticize anyone during the family meeting. Behavior, yes; the individual, never. In business, meeting rules are established: no lectures; no interrupting; no arguing; no raised voices; being passive-aggressive is not allowed. While these rules are fine in a business setting, they are not suitable for families. Notice that these are "what not to do" rules, they focus on the negative side of behavior.

In the family we want to shape our rules to be positive, uplifting, and detail what to do, rather than what not to do: keep it simple and keep it safe; we allow others to finish their thoughts; we listen; we share ideas; we speak in a pleasant manner; we are kind when we speak.

Do you see the difference? Remember to help your children focus on what to do more than on what not to do. Create your own family rules with these thoughts in mind.

When your Family Board Meetings are fun and safe, then you will see some wonderful things come from using this tool. If done right, it will be a supportive fun activity that your kids will demand you do. Laughter will become a common occurrence at your Family Board Meetings. Family relationships and family communication will drastically improve.

There is something special that happens when you introduce bottom-up communication and leadership into your home. Things will get accomplished easily, because you are empowering your children to take responsibility, openly communicate and share their feelings and opportunities they see for Continuous Family Improvement™. Over time your home life will be less stressful because of the improvements you are making together as a family. Give it a try, you'll love it.

JARED E. THATCHER

# SECTION 2:

## *The GATES™ Framework*

# CHAPTER 6

## Problem Solving with the GATES™ Framework

*A framework is simply a guide or a template for repeatable results. The GATES™ Framework is designed to help you problem solve any area of your family life you want to improve.*

The first part of this book was devoted to introducing you to a few of the principles of Lean and providing the foundational tool for Parenting the Lean Way – the Family Board. These Lean concepts and the Family Board will allow you to steer your own course to improvement within your family. They are the foundation for the framework of this book. If you embrace the ideas of adding value, eliminating waste, continuously improving, and valuing the individual, then you will have a mindset shift needed for Parenting the Lean Way.

The first part of this book provides you with the foundational knowledge of Lean principles and the instrument (the Family Board) for your family to steer its course; this second section is about how to chart and navigate your family's course. This second part is devoted to the problem solving and the Continuous Family

Improvement™ system found in the GATES™ framework and the tools associated with it.

To move in the direction you want to go, you need to open the gate and take that first step to the improvement that is critical to your personal growth and your family's happiness. The beauty of our humanity is that we can choose our destiny. Conversely, the great tragedy of humanity is that some people do not believe that they have anything special to share with the world. They don't believe they have a hand in making their own destiny. They don't try. They don't grow. Sadly, they deprive from us what they could have achieved, if only they had believed in their own potential. I believe that everyone can change.

I developed this system to make it easy for you to make change simple. It is based on my management consulting and business experience and my application of it at home with my family. I have taught this system to families around the world. This problem-solving framework has helped families to solve conflicts and issues, and continuously improve their home life. This framework is a simple template that will help you get repeatable results through using various tools and methods. These tools and the GATES™ framework will help make your life easier.

In the business world, practitioners of Lean often use a framework developed by the father of quality management, W. Edwards Deming, known as the PDSA cycle (Plan, Do, Study, Act). The PDSA cycle is used to make improvements and solve problems. You simply *plan* how you are going to fix a problem; you *do* the corrective actions; *study* the results of your solution on the problem; and *act* on any adjustments that need to be made. Then you repeat the cycle until the you have reached your improvement goals.

As simple as the PDSA cycle is for solving problems, there are two flaws that commonly occur when trying to implement this cycle. The first is in how it is utilized. PDSA is often used in emergencies to solve a problem rather using it proactively. As a result, the effort is focused on putting out a fire. They are focused on solving immediate needs, not looking for long-term solutions. People often fail to grasp the true root cause(s) of the problem in this firefighting mode. Instead they only put a band-aid on the symptom, never really solving the problem.

It's like applying anti-itch cream every time you develop a rash, it only provides temporary relief. Realizing that you develop a rash every time you eat a strawberry is identifying the root cause. If you stop eating strawberries, you never need the anti-itch cream again because you never develop another rash.

The second issue with the implementation of the PDSA cycle is that after developing a solution, people often fail to make sure that the solution they developed is used again in the future. Therefore, the problem was never really solved if you never formalize the solution. They are doomed to repeat the process.

The GATES™ framework accounts for these two implementation issues and incorporates change management throughout the process to help ensure that the improvements take place. It was also designed specifically with families in mind, to help them solve problems and continuously improve.

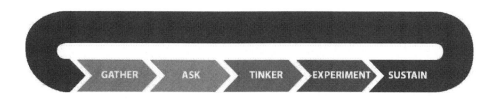

### GATES™ - The PROBLEM-SOLVING framework

The GATES™ framework is a problem-solving methodology. This five-phase framework stands for: *Gather, Ask, Tinker, Experiment, and Sustain.* Each phase is designed to guide you through successfully analyzing and solving your problems and issues. It can be used individually or collaboratively by parents, children, or the whole family. In the subsequent parts of Section Two of this book, each part will present several business tools that can help you achieve the objectives of that phase of this problem-solving framework. The five phases of the GATES™ framework are covered at a high level here:

**GATHER Phase:**

Just like it sounds, the GATHER Phase is all about gathering basic information about the problem or situation that needs improvement. There is a preparatory stage where you need to know what your Family Values are. This is important because these values will help influence your decisions about the priority of what to improve. This phase of the framework is focused on first identifying what you want to improve. Second, gathering basic information on what the problem or situation is, so that you can really understand at a high level what the contributing factors are.

When solving a problem, don't skip this first step of understanding the situation. If you do, you might end up addressing symptoms instead of curing the root cause of the problem. When you see the whole picture and grasp the situation, you have a better chance of being able to improve it.

In the GATHER Phase of this book you will find several tools that will help you gather information to better understand the problem. These tools will help you understand the current and future state of your family, create common values, and establish a family identity to help focus your efforts for improvement.

**ASK Phase:**

Once the problem has been identified, the next step is to start asking specific questions to get to the heart of the issue and find solutions to the problem. As I mentioned before, people often try to fix the symptoms of a problem without solving the problem's actual root cause. This phase takes the most time and has the most tools associated with it, because it is at this inquiry and planning stage that we uncover the real causes.

While no one wants to admit it to themselves, *you* might actually be a root cause of the problem and not even realize it. This phase gives *you* the opportunity to explore and really understand any given situation. It also gives *you* time to come to an acceptance that it might be *you* that is contributing to the root cause of the issues you are facing.

The tools you will find in the ASK Phase focus on getting to the root cause of the problem, exploring and documenting the problem in a visual way, developing solutions that add value to the family, and planning out a way to make sure that the changes you want to implement, happen.

### TINKER Phase:

Now that the root cause of the problem is identified and you have a plan on how to solve your issue, this is the phase when you start to tinker around with the solutions you developed to see what works and what doesn't. In the TINKER Phase you see if your solutions work.

What are possible solutions? How should you prioritize them? How can you track your improvements and hold yourself and others accountable? Who should be involved in making sure your solutions are implemented? These are some of the questions you'll answer as you make your improvements. This is about finalizing your improvement plan and implementing it. The Family Board and the Mini Sprint™ are the tools to help you organize and make sure you are working your improvement plan.

**EXPERIMENT Phase:**

This phase is fun, because you get to see your hard work paying off, as things begin to improve for the better! The EXPERIMENT Phase is where you test your action plan from the TINKER Phase to see what's working and what isn't. Just like an experiment in a lab, you monitor, measure, and track if your potential improvement is or isn't working. If it's not working, or there are unintended consequences to your actions, then you either start over, or make slight adjustments to get you to where you want to be. You hold people accountable to the commitments they made, and you learn from both your successes and your failures. I will show you a tool that has been used to help companies turn around their performance, teams to get motivated, and it will help you and your family to visually stay focused and accountable for making sure you achieve a positive solution.

**SUSTAIN Phase:**

The final phase, really isn't the final phase at all. The SUSTAIN Phase is all about standardizing your improvements and repeating the process all over again. This phase is here to ensure that you finish the last 1% of your solution and take the next step forward to fulfill the 'continuous' part of Continuous Family Improvement™. So many improvement projects fail to resolve their problems because they don't put the time into using the tools to standardize the improvement(s) that have been made, share their success stories, and start the process over. If you fail to complete this final 1% of your effort to your problem solving, you will repeatedly be trying to solve the same problem over and over again.

\* \* \*

Now that I've explained the conceptual part of this problem-solving framework, I feel it is important to present a practical example of how to use it. While this framework might seem complicated at first, it really is simple. To see how to use the GATES™ framework, here is how you might solve a typical issue that many parents face – children misbehaving to get their way.

This example comes from a good friend of mine from Nigeria. His children are generally well behaved, although he insists that they can be "something else" when he is wanting to sit down to watch a football (soccer) match and they want to watch cartoons. Generally, he finds himself giving into their demands and watching the cartoons with them. He wishes that they wouldn't act that way when he wants to watch a game. So, how can the GATES™ framework be helpful?

First, he has already identified the problem he wants to work on, so now he needs to GATHER information about their behavior from a high-level. From his standpoint, he doesn't appreciate the way they behave when they are insisting on watching cartoons, and he wishes that they would have some consideration for him when he wants to relax by watching a game. From the children's standpoint, they don't enjoy football as much as cartoons, and they love it even more that their Dad spends time watching the cartoons with them. They enjoy explaining to him what's going on.

By looking at the situation from a high level, we can begin to realize what each party values. The children enjoy cartoons and spending time, any time, with their Dad. The father of course also greatly values spending time with his kids, which is why he often gives into their requests, even though they are misbehaving. But he also values consideration and relaxing while watching a good football match. We also learn what things they don't value or see as waste. The way in which the kids ask to watch cartoons (their behavior), clearly does not add value and is something the father wants to minimize.

With that understanding of the situation, it is time to move into the ASK phase to really understand the root causes, so you can improve the situation. Just like the name suggests, *ask* the kids what is going on (in the section on the ASK Phase you will learn about the various tools you can use to get to the root cause of the problem). As he asks questions of both the kids and himself, he came to the following realizations. First, the children have learned to behave in the way that he doesn't appreciate because they know that he will give in *if* they act that way. He also learned that they like playing football more than watching it. Second, it became clear that the thing that they all value the most is spending time together.

He then involved his children in the second part of the ASK Phase which is to take what you learned about the root cause issue(s) of the problem and develop a plan of action to correct the problem. Together he and his kids brainstormed some possible solutions, and came up with a plan of action. By working together on a solution, everybody has a feeling of ownership for the results and thus a stake in seeing that the implementation of their ideas are successful.

In the TINKER Phase, you try out the solutions you developed to see what works. To get the kids not to behave in their typical way of bugging their father until he gives in to their pleadings, they agreed to ask politely, and he agreed to let them watch cartoons when they politely ask. They practiced modeling the correct behavior before the next situation arose. If they started to behave in the old unacceptable way, then they knew in advance that they wouldn't be allowed to watch cartoons. To help make this easier, they also worked out a schedule as to the times they would watch which program as a family.

He also learned why they didn't enjoy watching football. They didn't feel they were that good at it, so naturally they didn't enjoy it that much. Plus, they didn't feel the same interaction with their dad, that they felt when they were explaining the cartoons to him. Understanding that everyone enjoyed spending time together, helped them craft a compromise. After every game they watched together, they would all go outside and spend at least half-an-hour practicing a play that they had seen in the game. This gave them additional quality time together as they had fun, got some exercise, and learned some new football skills.

The EXPERIMENT Phase helped them to visually track what was working for them. They wrote down their schedule in advance, so there wouldn't be any arguments. They decided to track how often they played football together, and later they started tracking skill improvements.

Once things were working well for them, in the SUSTAIN Phase they wrote down and shared their success story with the whole family during the Family Board Meeting. They made sure that everyone was aware of how they had solved the problem and modified their behavior in a way that was acceptable. They talked about how they had identified which values were important to them, like spending time together and consideration for one another. Finally, they talked about how they could improve their relationship further, by starting the GATES™ framework over again and choosing something else to work on improving – in this case they started working on improving their football fundamental skills.

This problem and the solution might seem basic, but many of the issues and frustrations that happen within families are subtle. This is not a complicated problem-solving framework. It works because it helps make visible the issues we want to improve. The Lean and business tools you are about to learn are likewise simple to use.

\* \* \*

Here in section two of this book, you will be shown each of the five phases of the GATES™ framework. It will provide you with Lean business tools that can help you achieve the objective of that phase. Don't feel like you need to use each tool, or that these are the only tools available to you. In my on-line course and my week-long family retreats, I go into more depth with dozens of additional tools. This book will give you a good idea of how these business tools can help you as a parent.

Think what this could do in your family if you were always striving to be a better parent, spouse, child, or sibling? People notice when you change for the better and your efforts to improve the family will be rewarded. Parenting the Lean Way is about teaching your family how to achieve the things everyone wants to improve to reach your desired results. Following this simple GATES™ framework will help your family to grow into that potential you know is possible.

# CHAPTER 7

## How to Ensure that Change Happens

*In business, change management is essential in making sure that projects are adopted by the organization. This chapter on change is included to help you develop plans to overcome any resistance to the improvements you want to make in your home.*

In business, an entire discipline has developed around figuring out how to successfully manage change, mitigate the risks, remove obstacles, and motivate and re-train people to change the way they do things. One of the hardest things a company can do is to attempt to change its culture. Change Management is the solution.

Typically, this is used in business mergers and acquisitions – similar to any couple entering into marriage or starting a blended family. From the family context, you are attempting to change or merge family cultures and there will be resistance. Change management is also needed when you try and change the status quo of the family, especially when you try and improve. The resistance to this change may come from your children, and believe it or not, some of it may come from you.

The following are some of the main factors that contribute to resistance to change:

1. Aversion to leaving the status quo (comfort zone)
2. Inconsistent messaging
3. Misunderstandings about the reason(s) for the change
4. Lack of buy-in from all parties
5. No compelling vision
6. Low trust
7. Failure to reward successes
8. Absence of accountability
9. Unwillingness to change existing mental models
10. Little understanding around the derailers of change

The beauty of the GATES™ system is that it addresses the road blocks and distractions to implementing changes before you begin your improvement plan. When you develop countermeasures for the resistance to change before you begin your improvements, you will have a greater chance for a successful implementation.

In this chapter we will look at these resistance factors one at a time. Take the time to answer each question. Really contemplate how these resistance factors could affect you or your children. Your answers will become part of your final roadmap for the continuous family improvements you desire in your life.

## 1. Aversion to Leaving the Status Quo (current state or your comfort zone)

The status quo is "safe" because it is what we know. For each of us, to some degree or another, the unknown creates fear, uncertainty, and stress. We may not like our current state, but at least we know what it is. It's this kind of attitude that will cause us to stick to the way things are and resist change. This is a form of procrastination. Especially when we say to ourselves, "Well, the old way isn't *soooo* bad." Never allow yourself or others to justify staying in this "safe" place, because it prevents you from obtaining your true goal, your higher purpose, and the vision of the future state you really desire.

An exception to this procrastination and resistance to change is if the status quo is so undesirable that anything would be better. Hopefully, this won't be your predicament. But if it is, there is hope, and on the bright side, it will be easier to implement change with this motivation driving you.

What don't you like about the status quo? (Refer to behaviors and attitudes, not individuals)

_____

_____

Why do you want to make a change?

_____

_____

What is your motivation for making a change?

_____

_____

## 2. Inconsistent Messaging

It is essential that you have a consistent message of what and why you are changing. Children should never hear their parents offer anything but the same message. Good cop/bad cop might work fine in the movies, but within the home, such a strategy undermines the authority of the other. This doesn't mean that parents can't disagree, but such disagreements should be handled in private.

It is far better to agree beforehand as to what the family is working for, why the change is important, and what the rewards and consequences should be. When you try and come up with something on the spur of the moment you might say something that can be seen as contradictory to what the other parent has said.

Nothing derails change faster than not being able to stay consistent in the message of the what and why the change should happen. Provide a clear roadmap and this will ease the apprehension of those going through the change. This system will help you craft that message so you can be clear with what the purpose is, how you will measure the improvement, and the action steps needed to make the improvements.

What areas in your life have you experienced inconsistent messaging?

_____

_____

What can you do at home to align the messages you give?

_____

_____

### 3. Misunderstandings about the Reason(s) for the Change.

Reasons will vary for why people decided to buy this book, but everyone's final goal is to improve the family from where it is now to where you want it to be. However, how you introduce this transformation to your family can be a major impediment to the success of your transformation. If you are not aware of how it might be perceived by your children or even your spouse, disaster could await.

"Hey kids/spouse, I've found this great program that is going to help our family improve the way we do things!" That might sound good to you, but what your kids or spouse might misinterpret it as, "Hey you rotten kids/spouse, because we are having so many problems, I am going to force you to sit through this program to change you!" Don't allow misinterpretations like this to derail you before you even start.

How might the way you present this program be interpreted by the other family members?

_____

_____

Who is likely to most misunderstand the reason for change? and why?

_____

_____

What do you think you can do to prevent these misunderstandings?

_____

_____

### 4. Lack of Buy-in from All Parties

If anyone is resistant to making the change, they will create a roadblock not only for themselves but for others who are trying to embrace the system. How do you minimize or eliminate this resistance? The GATES™ System will provide the opportunities to actively engage all members of your family in this journey.

I will show you how to not only bring your family along for the journey, but also how to turn the controls over to them to actively participate in the navigation. You will see children become more committed to this system, in some cases, more than the parents who introduced them to it. This happens because the children will feel empowered to make changes that last when they feel like they are contributing to the successes in the family. Now that's powerful!

You will shortly see how the GATES™ System will provide ways to get buy-in from all family members. The workshops from the GATHER Phase will actively seek your family members' feedback and ask for their opinions. The ASK Phase, likewise, will include your family in finding the root cause of issues. This active inclusion and participation in developing solutions makes the action plan theirs. They helped create it, so they have a vested interest in seeing it succeed.

What might be your reason(s) that prevent you from allowing your children to contribute and develop solutions to family problems?

_____

_____

If this is the case, how will you overcome your hesitancy to give responsibility to your children?

_____

_____

### 5. No Compelling Vision

Why do you want to try this system? What are the guiding principles and values in your life? What do you as a family stand for and want to accomplish? If you don't already have your family's values written down, Chapter 9 will help you develop them for your family. This will help align your family with a common vision and provide the step you will need to have all the members of your family focused on the compelling vision you all created together.

When you know why you want to change, when you have a clear vision of where you want to go, then there is power behind your actions. It is like having the wind in your sails to propel you forward. Without a compelling vision, you have no wind to fill your sails, no reason to help you change.

What is your compelling vision for change, which you and your whole family can get behind and support?

_____

_____

Is there anyone that this compelling vision might not resonate with? What might help motivate them?

_____

_____

### 6. Low Trust

Have you ever put your family through a program before, or tried to implement an idea and then failed to follow through with it? If you have, and we've all been there, then from the standpoint of your family this is just another flavor of the month that will be doomed to failure.

In business, managers who find themselves in this situation have two tools they can use to quickly rebuild trust with their employees. They can either hire a consulting firm to show they are serious about implementing the change, and/or as a last resort they can fire a dissenter to illustrate their determination for making the change happen. Clearly this doesn't work in a family setting, because you can't fire your children (although there might be times we might wish we could with teenagers).

Fortunately, there are other methods to rebuild the trust you have with your family. Determination and commitment to follow through to completion on what you say you'll do are big parts of rebuilding trust. Time is the another.

How might you have lowered the trust your spouse or children have with you?

_____

_____

What are you willing to commit to do to rebuild the trust they have in you?

_____

_____

## 7. Failure to Reward Successes

Money is not the only motivating factor in job satisfaction nor is it ranked the highest, especially with Millennials. Relationships with co-workers and supervisors, having fun, having a job that has purpose, and being recognized for successes, are all factors in job satisfaction. Likewise, recognizing and rewarding successes made by your family members will help cement with positive affirmation "right" behaviors they have made in their continuous improvement efforts.

Just to be clear, I am not suggesting that you should reward your children, or yourself, for *everything* they/you do. We don't want to enable our children or have them become dependent on praise. What I am suggesting, is that from the standpoint of making changes, which are often uncomfortable, providing a special reward is appropriate. We need to praise our kids for the challenging work that they do. Our kids should know that we are proud of them, but that praise should mean something and not be a throwaway greeting we give them any time they do something.

What are some rewards that might incentivize your family? What motivates them?

---

---

## 8. Absence of Accountability

This one step, if ignored, can lead to procrastination faster than anything else. If you fail to hold your daily Family Board Meetings (see Chapter 5), then this system won't work. Consistency is the key to success. The best way to ensure consistency in this system is to measure actions and hold yourself and others accountable. Refuse to accept any excuse for not following through. Chapter 16 will cover how to create visual accountability through Key Performance Indicators (KPIs).

What does accountability look like for you?

_____

_____

Who do you want to be accountable to for following this system? and why?

_____

_____

## 9. Unwillingness to Change Existing Mental Models

All of us see the world through our own eyes, based on our own experiences and paradigms. Resistance to change, or the failure to accept a new idea, comes from an unwillingness to adjust the prescription of one's mental glasses. If you refuse to accept the possibility that new ideas, or ideas that might even run counter to your current belief system, could offer solutions to help you change for the better, then you miss out on something that could positively impact your life. This unrealistic desire to stay in the status quo can prevent you from growth.

If you are having trouble with your vision, and after seeing the ophthalmologist, you refuse to accept the new prescription because you are comfortable with the way things are, then you miss the ability to see clearly. No one who gets an ophthalmologist prescription says, "How dare you say there is something wrong with me! I'm fine! It's the world that's blurry and has nothing to do with me!" That may seem laughable, but this is a big reason people fail to change.

To change, means you must admit to yourself, at least on some level, that you are doing something wrong. That's never an easy thing to admit. Sometimes the problem might lie with us and not others. That can be a challenging thing to accept. But just like the ophthalmologist prescription, the ideas, tools, methods, and systems found in this book are not a condemnation of you, but an opportunity to see the world clearer. Please be willing to try and see what works for you and your family. Continuous Family Improvement™ is a mental model we all need to accept to see the world with clarity.

Is it easy for you to admit when you are wrong? Why or why not?

_____

_____

What can you do to humble yourself and take responsibility to admit when you are wrong?

_____

_____

Who in your family might have a hard time admitting that they might need to change? What can you do to help them?

_____

_____

Have you ever made an assumption about a family member that wasn't correct? Why did you make that assumption?

_____

_____

How might you be willing to suspend negative assumptions about family members?

_____

_____

### 10. Little Understanding Around the Derailers of Change

Anytime we attempt to make a change in the way we do things, we are in essence rewiring our brain to create a new habit. With proper motivation, it's relatively easy to make immediate improvements and follow a new system, but over time we tend to revert back to our old habits.

In psychology terms, chances are good that you will experience a "spontaneous recovery." In other words, a testing of the system might result in a return to past behavior. For a few days, things might be going great, and then there will be a test to the new system. Persevere through this first test and things will improve for a few days to even a week or two, but then comes the big test where things will appear to deteriorate, perhaps even worse than before you began the change. This is the start of the spontaneous recovery (a correction back to old habits). If you are aware of it, and know it is normal, then it's not a surprise and you can deal with it successfully.

In Jeanie Daniel Duck's book, _The Change Monster_ [xii], she describes the importance of being ready to handle these derailers as a key to any successful change initiative. The awareness that something is wrong might come just before or in conjunction with a crisis. Most people take a crisis as justification for abandoning the change and returning to a form of the old status quo.

The same can be true in your family. If you know that a reoccurrence of old behaviors will come, then you aren't surprised, and you can get through any derailer that might threaten the change. Stay on course and don't abandon the system at the first sign of it not working. Stick with it and you will find that the change will happen.

Describe a time when you might have experienced a "spontaneous recovery" when you tried something new?

_____

_____

What happened to the change you were trying to achieve after this experience?

_____

_____

What are you going to do next time you notice a "spontaneous recovery" occurring?

_____

_____

Describe how committed you are to ensure that you stick to the system despite course corrections, back slides, and "spontaneous recoveries" you experience?

_____

_____

\* \* \*

If you think back to any resistance you have experienced when you have tried to change something, you should be able to tie it back to one or more of the change resistance factors I've outlined here. Now that you have a better understanding about several of the resistance factors to change, you are better equipped as a parent to make sure that your family's improvement projects have the best chance of success. You now have in your parenting tool box invaluable resources that will help you to improve your family and deal with change.

As you develop a strategy to improve anything you want through the GATES™ framework, make sure to address these typical change resistance factors, so that you will have effective countermeasures to deploy. You need to be prepared if any of them arise. This is where most parents go wrong when they try to improve any aspect of their family, they fail to account for the resistance to change which they will be met with. You, however, are now prepared for them and ready for success!

> *"Change your thoughts*
> *and you change your world."*
> *- Norman Vincent Peale*

*"One reason people resist change is
because they focus on what they have to give up,
instead of what they have to gain."*
                              *- Seth Godwin*

# SECTION 2:

## *The GATES™ Framework - GATHER*

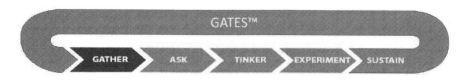

**OBJECTIVES:**

**1.** Use your goals, values, and purpose as an individual or a family to direct your decision on the area of improvement to focus on.

**2.** Identify the area you want to improve.

**3.** Don't assume. Gather an overall understanding of your area of improvement.

# CHAPTER 8

## Understanding Current State/Future State with a Family Focus Group

*The first step to the GATHER phase is to understand your current state and know what you want your future state to be. You can then identify the gap between the two and develop a strategy to get you there.*

When my wife asked me what business tools could help the family at home, the Family Board was the first tool that came to mind, a Family Focus Group was second. This tool is presented in the GATHER Phase of the GATES™ framework because it serves to help you understand generally how people feel about the way things are and the way they wish it could be. A Focus Group in a family setting helps you determine how your family sees both its current state and its ideal future state. This is a fun tool that your family is really going to enjoy. I have used it at Daimler, at Nike, with my own family, and at all my parenting workshops with remarkable success.

What makes a Family Focus Group such a great tool? Well, it's the way you get at the true feelings of people in a non-threatening way. You do this by using pictures. I have seen children as young as four-years-old give an assessment of how they see the family that is as good as some adults describing something at the corporate level. Let me show you how this is done.

First, we need to have pictures available to spark the ideas that will help your family to relate their feelings to each other. There are two ways to do this. The first way is by far the easiest, but one I would recommend only if you don't have time or if your kids are unwilling participants. If this is the case, use the Visual Idea Cue Cards I have created for you (found in the Appendix).

The second way takes a little more effort, but one that will be a fun activity for your children, especially younger ones. Gather some old magazines you don't mind being cut up. The photos from the Visual Idea Cue Cards should give you an idea about the type of photos and magazines you are looking for.

Make an activity out of cutting out the pictures. Get the kids together and have them cut out the photos that they like. Enjoy the time you are cutting out the photos by engaging with your children. Ask your kids what pictures they like and why. You will learn things from their responses. Have fun creating your own photo collection while making memories at the same time.

Next, set a specific time to have your Family Focus Group. Evenings or weekends often work best. The activity will take about 45-60 minutes depending on the ages and size of your family. Make sure that the time is blocked out and you can do it uninterrupted. For materials, you will need the photos, sticky notes, markers, a place to post the photos with comments, a camera phone to take a picture of the results, and a print-out of the Future State Solutions Worksheet (found at the end of this chapter).

On the day of the focus group, gather the whole family together and explain that you are going to do a little exercise to first understand how everyone sees the family as it is today and then as they would like it to be.

Spread the photos out on the table and ask each family member to choose three photos that best describe for them what they think of the family today.

Give them a time limit to select the photos and write down their reason why they selected the photo. If you need to help the younger children with this, I recommend adding a little more time than the typical 10 minutes for this part of the activity. Be sure to let them know when five minutes remain, and one minute is left. This will help everyone to be on schedule.

Now there are a couple of rules I want you to explain to everyone prior to sharing their three choices.

The first rule is when someone is speaking everyone listens (this means that no one else interrupts, makes fun of, or belittles their contribution). It is okay to ask some clarifying questions about what they see in the photo to help you better understand what they are saying. It is best to wait until they are done sharing before asking any clarifying questions.

The second rule is that everyone participates. Don't, for example, exclude younger children because you think that they can't do this activity. You would be surprised at how well they can verbalize what they are feeling once they have the starting place of the photo to get them thinking and talking.

The final rule is that when sharing what the pictures mean to you, it is okay to talk about behavior, but do not associate the behavior with an individual. In other words, no one is allowed to target a family member for criticism. Don't do it! Keep the activity a safe place where no one feels like they have been directly attacked.

After explaining the rules, everyone will showcase what pictures they chose and why. Put the pictures on the wall, window, door, or whatever you are using, and stick it in place with the sticky note you used to write down a brief description of what the picture means to you. Model how to do this by showing your first picture, letting your family know why you chose that picture and how it relates to how you see the family today. Take turns going around the room until everyone has had an opportunity to contribute their three photos and explain their feelings about the family.

Once this is done, take a picture of the pictures with the explanations, making sure you can read what they wrote. This will help you remember in the future what your family perceived as the current state of your family at that point in time. Over time you can see how your family's current state perceptions have changed. Record what everyone said in the Future State Solutions Worksheet by recording it in the left-hand side under "Current State." You will use one sheet per person.

Now that you are done with the current state of the family, repeat the process for the ideal future state of the family. Ask them this question, "If anything were possible, what would you like our family to look and act like in an ideal future state?"

Again, repeat the process: Take 10 minutes to find your three pictures, writing why you chose your pictures on the sticky notes. Be sure to give a countdown so everyone knows how much time is left. Take turns finding out what everyone envisions their ideal family life to look like. Take a picture of the results of your family's ideal state.

Finally, discuss with the family any trends you noticed. What were the biggest surprises? What do they think you should work at improving together as a family first? Be sure to capture these ideas on the Future State Solutions Worksheet. This time you will write it down under the "Ideal Future State" on the right side of the page. Be sure to align that ideal family vision opposite its' corresponding current state reality.

For example, if someone said, "We don't raise our voices, and speak politely to each other in our family" for the ideal future state, you would write that opposite the current state example of, "Everyone argues with each other too much." If, on the other hand, there is no current state example to align up your ideal future state to, then you would write it down with nothing on the left hand current state side. For example, someone may have mentioned, "We have enough money to help other people," as an ideal future state. During the previous current state activity, if no one mentioned anything about money, finances, or giving to charity, then this suggestion would get its own section.

After you write everything down, review the Future State Solutions Worksheet and see if there are any current state examples that don't align with a corresponding ideal future state, and vice versa. It is easy enough to then fill in the blanks going either direction. Be sure to get involvement from the family when filling in the blanks.

This entire exercise should have taken around 45 minutes to an hour. My suggestion is that you then have a treat for the family to enjoy afterwards: ice cream, cookies, a board game, or whatever your family typically does as a reward. While you are enjoying the treat, take a minute and review the ideas you've recorded on the Future State Solutions Worksheets. Are you noticing any trends? If so, pick one, and see if everyone would like to work on fixing that issue. If you don't see anything that jumps out at you, then ask the kids what one thing they would like to work on.

The reason you are getting the kids to choose what to work on is that by them coming up with the area they want to work on improving, it becomes their idea. They picked it, and they now own it. They now have a vested interest in seeing their idea become successful. If you, as the parent, choose it and say, this is what we are doing, then they might rebel against the ultimatum. By letting them pick the area they want to work on, you are empowering them to make decisions and act for themselves. This is a powerful lesson to teach any child at any age – that when they see something that needs to get fixed, they can take responsibility for improving it. Empowering the family is a big part of what makes Parenting the Lean Way so different.

Ideally as a family you have picked out three ideal future states you would like to work on together. Next develop at least three action steps for each example that will get you bridge the gap from your current state to that ideal state. The reason you pick three comes from a coaching and mentoring tool known as the Rule of Three[xiii]. When trying to think of a solution there are always at least three. This forces you to think and when thinking past the obvious answers, that's generally when you become creative and you think of a win–win solution. You may even want to turn these action steps into a SMART Goal for your family to work on. Be sure to keep any goal, *S*pecific, *M*easurable, *A*chievable, *R*ealistic and *T*ime-bound.

Now a word of warning, don't start by picking an area that only one person needs to work on. Pick an area that the whole family needs to work on together. This is not to be used as an attack or to be vindictive. "Mom nags, so mom needs to work on that." Or "My brother bugs me, he needs to stop." Wrong! The right way would be "We are going to work at doing what mom asks us to do the first time so that she doesn't feel the need to nag." The right way would be "I'm going to do more things with my brother, so he doesn't have to get my attention by bugging me, while he will work on giving me space when I'm doing my homework or hanging out with my friends." I hope you can see the difference between attacking an individual and addressing a behavior so that everyone can help and participate in a solution.

Using the Family Focus Group to help identify areas of improvement can be beneficial to the whole family. Making our feelings visible helps us better understand each other and strive for improvements. Be sure to hang on to the Future State Solutions Worksheet because you are going to use them again in Chapter 12.

*"We worry about what a child will be tomorrow, yet we forget that he is someone today."*
*- Stacia Tauscher*

# The Future State Solutions Worksheet

IDENTIFY YOUR CURRENT STATE AND YOUR IDEAL FUTURE STATE - WHAT'S THE GAP?

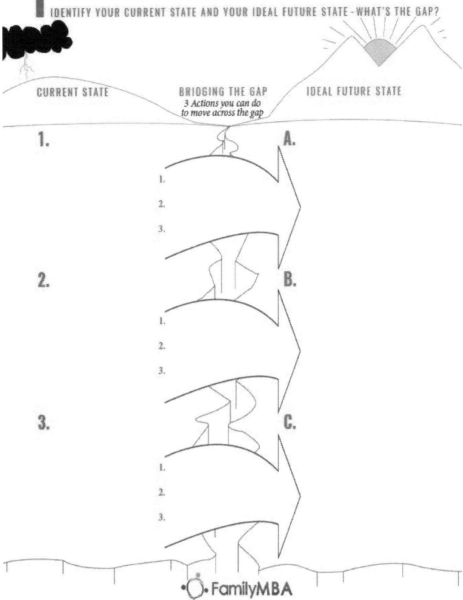

CURRENT STATE

BRIDGING THE GAP
3 Actions you can do
to move across the gap

IDEAL FUTURE STATE

1.

A.

1.

2.

3.

2.

B.

1.

2.

3.

3.

C.

1.

2.

3.

FamilyMBA

# CHAPTER 9

## The Gravity of Values – How They Impact Your Thoughts and Actions

*In the GATHER Phase, it is important to understand the motivations behind your actions. Have you ever thought about what your core values are? Do you know what your children's core values are? Let's find out.*

Most companies find it necessary to establish their company's core values. This acts as a way for the employees to know how to act and how to make decisions. This also helps customers understand and identify with companies of similar values. These published values also affect the culture of the company for good or for bad.

Likewise, all families have a core set of values, but in almost all cases they are unwritten. In this chapter, I am going to show you how to identify your core family values, because when our values are not documented, it is easy to get off course. Having them written down and prioritized helps you set a true course. They also offer a consistent foundation to refer to when we need to help correct our children's, and our own, wrong choices.

**Gravity of Values**

While working on my MBA dissertation, I developed a theory I call the "Gravity of Values." The Gravity of Values theory states that, "Most cultural behavior will be drawn to the value (stated or unstated) that the organization actually values."

To put this theory into context, I interviewed an executive from a well-known global firm. He provided a perfect example of this theory in action. One of the top stated values of this company was respecting the individual. However, there was a managing director at the firm who would routinely berate, yell, and throw things at employees. The executive I was talking to mentioned two observations: first, if he had behaved in that way, he would have been fired for violating the company's values statement. The only reason the other director was not terminated was that he brought in millions of dollars worth of business. Second, he observed that others in their company were starting to exhibit a mild form of this bad behavior, as these employees started to bring in money from their accounts.

This company cared more about generating revenue than respecting the individual. Because of how the managers acted, the employees realized that making money was more important to the company than valuing the individual—despite what the firm said they valued, their actions spoke louder. This resulted in a lack of trust for management by exposing their hypocrisy, and the culture of their organization began to change, becoming toxic. It was drawn into a cycle where improving the bottom line was more important than respect for colleagues. The culture had changed.

Likewise, in a family, we might say that we care about certain values, but our actions as parents can make hypocrites out of us. Our children inherently are drawn through the Gravity of Values to those things that we actually care about. We can't parent by telling our children to do as I say, not as I do. Actions truly speak louder than words. If we want a loving, respectful, and caring "culture" in our homes, our adherence to those values needs to be actively demonstrated by us, the parents.

In most cases, if a child is behaving in a way that we do not condone, chances are we have created an opening for another value to have a greater impact on them. How often do we yell at our children, and yet we repeatedly tell them to be respectful and courteous to each other and that yelling is not okay? Do we break up a sibling fight and tell them to be kinder to each other (adding value), and yet when we come home from work, do we reach out to our spouse or our kids to do kind things for them? Remember the Gravity of Values theory, the frustration you feel from your child's misbehavior may stem from the inconsistencies of your actions.

Values are the core principles and beliefs that guide us in the decisions that we make, and influence the actions we take. Our children's core beliefs are initially learned from us. Having the "right" values makes it easier for us as parents to teach our children how to behave. Have you established those core beliefs in your home for your children? Only you can answer that question. By looking at the actions and belief system of your family, you will have a clearer vision of what's working and what isn't.

As parents, we are not the only ones that can teach our children. The world is also trying to impose its values on our children. Establishing clear values early in our children's development is important in order to fortify them against the competing values that your family may not agree with.

If you want to change the dynamic of your family life, you must first understand what values truly matter to your family. Then you need to adopt and prioritize the values that will give you the results you are seeking. Finally, to make a change, you must live those values by example. If you want to change your actions, then you first need to change the priority of your values that influence those actions.

Having your Core Family Values written down can be a powerful tool when talking with our children. When they misbehave, you can have a discussion (not an argument) with them about how their behavior didn't align with your family's core value. A discussion, a two-way conversation, is far more effective than losing your temper at misbehavior. This conversation is only possible if you have written down your Core Family Values and your children know them.

**Steps for Creating Core Family Values:**

**1.** Make it a special occasion. If your kids feel there is a special significance attached to this event, then they will know that it is important.

**2.** Set a time to have a planning session with the entire family. Ask them to think about what core values your family exhibits or should exhibit. See the Values Brainstorming List toward the end of this chapter to give you some ideas about values you can choose (it's obviously not a complete list).

**3.** Get participation from everyone. Collect everyone's thoughts about what family values matter most. Do this by asking two questions:

**a.** "What's most important to you in our family life?"

**b.** "What else?" keep repeating this question until you cannot think of anything else.

**4.** Narrow down the values you want to keep. I suggest no more than a dozen. If you can memorize your Core Family Values, then it is easier to concentrate on embracing and internalizing them.

**5.** Take time to prioritize the values. The Values Matrix is a great tool for prioritizing your values. (see the example worksheet at the end of this chapter)

**6.** Write out your Family Values in order of importance.

**7.** Print and refer to your Family Value Statement often.

When your Core Family Values are written down you can see if any of your values conflict with any of your other values. For example, if success at work is more important than valuing a family member's time, you should definitely re-evaluate those values. By prioritizing your values, you have that opportunity to see if any of them are a potential road block, creating conflicts with where you want to be, or how you want to be. Seeing these misalignments allows you to change your values and beliefs to reflect those values that should matter the most.

Prioritizing your Core Family Values helps you make decisions that are right for your family. I suggest you do this exercise both individually and as a family. Compare how everyone ranked their individual values. Their lists might surprise you, and more importantly, help you understand why you might be having conflicts with family members. Does their prioritization of their values conflict with your values? From that starting point, you can work together at redefining what is important to your family and find common ground.

When I say "redefining," I don't mean you set an ultimatum on what you should all value. This should be a collaborative effort. You want everyone to feel that their input was valued and appreciated. You are a family, and as such you work together to reach a consensus and define what matters most to all of you.

When parents marry, they each come together having been brought up with their own distinct set of values they learned from their parents. Even if those values are similar, how many conflicts are the result of a different prioritization of each of their value systems?

To give you an idea about what core values can look like, here's a little case study for helping you develop your own Core Family Values. It is taken from the Boy Scouts of America, who refer to their values as the Scout Law.

I earned my Eagle Scout rank over twenty-five years ago, and I can still remember the Scout Law without needing to read it:

> *"A Scout is trustworthy, loyal, helpful, friendly, courteous, kind, obedient, cheerful, thrifty, brave, clean, and reverent."*

Although as boys, we typically added a thirteenth one: hungry.

To give you another idea on how you might want to list the values that are important to you, here is another example. This time from the Scout Association in the United Kingdom. Their Scout values are:

> *"As Scouts we are guided by these values:*
> *Integrity - We act with integrity; we are honest, trustworthy and loyal.*
> *Respect - We have self-respect and respect for others.*
> *Care - We support others and take care of the world in which we live.*
> *Belief - We explore our faiths, beliefs and attitudes.*
> *Co-operation - We make a positive difference; we co-operate with others and make friends."*

The reason I presented these two examples for how to write out your core values is because even though they are the same basic global organization, each country organization has developed their own unique value statement.

You can either list your values individually or define what each value means with their precepts spelled out for your family. The point is there is no "right" way to do it. The important thing is that you simply create your own Core Family Values together. Do what works for your family. When you work together to craft your core values, they will be meaningful and unique to your family.

Another tip would be to keep the list short. Although BSA has a dozen values, almost too many to remember – it is possible. All Scouts are required to memorize the Scout Law to get their first rank advancement. They can typically learn it in less than an hour. They repeat it at every meeting to make sure it sticks. Thirty years after first learning the Scout Law, I can still quote it without having to think about it. Scouts are constantly taught what these values mean. The leaders, both the boys and the adults, refer to them often to reinforce to the Scouts the significance of these values and how to properly act by implementing them into their lives.

Your family can do a similar thing, in which your children will remember your family values for years to come. It will be a moral compass for them throughout their lives and will help shape their character. It will reduce conflicts and help you become a better family. What an incredible gift! Please take the time to do this activity together as a family! Be sure to use your Core Family Values every day during your Family Board Meeting. You'll be glad you did.

# The Values Matrix.

PRIORITIZE YOUR VALUES TO UNDERSTAND WHAT MATTERS MOST TO YOUR FAMILY

## An Example of our Worksheet

I've grayed out value #1's winning match up with the other values. In the first match up we see that value #2 won, but value #1 beat value #3 in the second match up. Total all the wins, and in this case, value #1 won three match ups.

Finally, you record the total points that each value received and rank them by order of importance.

### VALUES RANKED:

1. Charity
2. Integrity
3. Faith
4. Forgiveness
5. Leadership
6. Self-Control  — Tie with 5 votes each. In the match up: Self-Control beat Loyalty.
7. Loyalty
8. Excellence
9. Learning
10. Fitness
11. Happiness
12. Serenity

Fitness — Value #1
Faith — Value #2
Happiness — Value #3
Loyalty — Value #4
Learning — Value #5
Self-Control — Value #6
Integrity — Value #7
Serenity — Value #8
Charity — Value #9
Forgiveness — Value #10
Excellence — Value #11
Leadership — Value #12

THATCHER FAMILY VALUES
We exemplify the values of... Faith Charity Integrity Forgiveness Leadership Loyalty
We are in the pursuit of... Excellence Self-Control Knowledge Health & Fitness Happiness Serenity
and Financial Freedom

| Total #1 | Total #2 | Total #3 | Total #4 | Total #5 | Total #6 | Total #7 | Total #8 | Total #9 | Total #10 | Total #11 | Total #12 |
|---|---|---|---|---|---|---|---|---|---|---|---|
| 3 | 9 | 2 | 5 | 3 | 5 | 9 | 0 | 11 | 8 | 4 | 7 |

•◇• FamilyMBA

# The Values Matrix.

PRIORITIZE YOUR VALUES TO UNDERSTAND WHAT MATTERS MOST TO YOUR FAMILY

VALUES RANKED:

1. _____
2. _____
3. _____
4. _____
5. _____
6. _____
7. _____
8. _____
9. _____
10. _____
11. _____
12. _____

Value #1
Value #2
Value #3
Value #4
Value #5
Value #6
Value #7
Value #8
Value #9
Value #10
Value #11
Value #12

Total #1 | Total #2 | Total #3 | Total #4 | Total #5 | Total #6 | Total #7 | Total #8 | Total #9 | Total #10 | Total #11 | Total #12

# The Values Brainstorming List.

A SHORT LIST OF VALUES TO GET YOU STARTED THINKING ABOUT WHAT MATTERS

- Accountability
- Accuracy
- Achievement
- Adventurousness
- Altruism
- Ambition
- Assertiveness
- Balance
- Being the best
- Belonging
- Boldness
- Brave
- Calmness
- Carefulness
- Challenge
- Charity
- Cheerfulness
- Clear-mindedness
- Commitment
- Community
- Compassion
- Competitiveness
- Consistency
- Contentment
- Continuous Improvement
- Contribution
- Control
- Cooperation
- Correctness
- Courtesy
- Creativity
- Curiosity
- Decisiveness
- Democraticness
- Dependability
- Determination
- Devoutness
- Dignity
- Diligence

- Discipline
- Discretion
- Diversity
- Dynamism
- Economy
- Effectiveness
- Efficiency
- Elegance
- Empathy
- Enjoyment
- Enthusiasm
- Equality
- Excellence
- Excitement
- Expertise
- Exploration
- Expressiveness
- Fairness
- Faith
- Family-orientedness
- Fidelity
- Fitness
- Fluency
- Focus
- Forgiving
- Freedom
- Friendly
- Fun
- Generosity
- Goodness
- Grace
- Growth
- Happiness
- Hard Work
- Health
- Helping Society
- Holiness
- Honesty
- Honor

- Humility
- Independence
- Ingenuity
- Inner Harmony
- Inquisitiveness
- Insightfulness
- Integrity
- Intelligence
- Intellectual Status
- Intuition
- Joy
- Justice
- Knowledge
- Leadership
- Learning
- Legacy
- Love
- Loyalty
- Making a difference
- Mastery
- Merit
- Obedience
- Openness
- Order
- Originality
- Patriotism
- Perfection
- Piety
- Positivity
- Practicality
- Preparedness
- Professionalism
- Prudence
- Punctual
- Quality-orientation
- Reliability
- Resourcefulness
- Respectful
- Results-oriented

- Reverant
- Rigor
- Security
- Self-actualization
- Self-control
- Selflessness
- Self-reliance
- Sensitivity
- Serenity
- Service
- Shrewdness
- Simplicity
- Soundness
- Speed
- Spontaneity
- Stability
- Strategic
- Strength
- Structure
- Success
- Support
- Teamwork
- Temperance
- Thankfulness
- Thoroughness
- Thoughtfulness
- Thrifty
- Timeliness
- Tolerance
- Traditionalism
- Trustworthiness
- Truth-seeking
- Understanding
- Uniqueness
- Unity
- Usefulness
- Valiant
- Vision
- Vitality

# CHAPTER 10

## The Family Coat of Arms –
## The Original Brand Management

*Brand Management creates value for a company. It tells a story about what the brand stands for, what it believes in, and the value it provides. Create that same brand recognition with your family name and family history to inspire your children.*

In this modern age, we are all familiar with the business concept of the brand. It's everywhere. It has been estimated that we are bombarded with between 4,000 and 10,000 types of advertising and branding messages every day[xiv]. With that kind of advertising hitting our kids daily, what are we doing to provide a positive 'branding' of our own families to them?

Did you realize that originally the brand was used by families, not by businesses? A brand is about reputation. For families that brand was seen in the form of a coat of arms. It was used to show status, what values the family held dear, and to highlight accomplishments they had obtained. It was only later that business adopted branding and then dominated its use.

A unifying family tool that you can create is your own Family Brand, in the form of your own family crest. You are going to take back from business the concept of the brand and use it with your family.

What will this accomplish?

It's going to bring together what we have done previously in identifying your Core Family Values to create a visual representation of what your family believes and stands for. It will increase the pride in your family, and be a symbol of what you strive to become as a family.

In business, the company logo represents their products and services. There are well respected brands in business: Apple, Nike, Mercedes, Armani, and the list goes on. You see their logo and you immediately recognize what they do, what they value, and their quality. I want your Family Coat of Arms to have that kind of respect and recognition in your own home – to command that reputation you want your family to have associated with it. It's time for families to take back the concept of branding and use it to create pride within their family.

Daimler, famous for the Mercedes Benz brand, is one such company where brand management is very important to them. It is their image, and they are highly protective of it. I remember having a conversation at dinner with one of the company's executives a few years ago. I told him how when we first moved to Scotland, our boys (eight and five at the time) commented to me that the people must be rich in Scotland. I asked them why they thought they were rich? They looked at me like I was crazy and said, "Dad, even the garbage trucks are Mercedes!" Referring to the Daimler star on the truck's grill. As young as my boys were, they recognized the logo and they knew the reputation of the brand.

The executive laughed at that story and told me that while they were initially concerned that having their logo on trucks might devalue the brand, after careful consideration they felt the brand would be an asset for their truck and bus division. And they were right.

As your family creates your Family Brand, or a coat of arms, I want you to also treat your Family Brand Management with that same kind of respect and consideration. This Family Coat of Arms will be the visual representation of your family values, vision, and beliefs, so treat it with that same respect. Make your brand management mean something to your family. Make it special.

One of my passions is family history. I love reading ancestors' stories and learning their backgrounds. In fact, one of my great-grandfathers, Edmond Moodye, in 1540 was granted a coat of arms for saving King Henry the VIII's life. I'm sure a few of Henry's wives resented that act of heroism. The symbolism found in his coat of arms helps tell the story of that event. His personal brand was forever associated with that event.

The Arms and Crest of Edmond Moodye
otherwise Moody of Bury St. Edmunds in the County of
Suffolk, A gentleman granted by letters patent under
the hand and Seal of Thomas Hawley Clarenceux
King of Arms the sixth day of October 1540.

College of Arms
London

Windsor Herald of Arms.

I bring up family history because *The New York Times* did a story where they said, "The more children know about their family's history, the stronger their sense of control over their lives, the higher their self-esteem and the more successfully they believed their families functioned[xv]." The research sited in the article suggested that the biggest single predictor of a child's emotional health and happiness was correlated to how well they knew their family's stories.

This is one of the reasons why creating a Family Coat of Arms is going to help your family. It helps your children know something about their family. It will inspire them and improve their self-confidence. They will have pride in the reputation of their family.

So, how do you create it? In this explanation I'm going to be using the traditional coat of arms; the Japanese Kamon or family crest, a family seal, emblem, flag or banner will work just as well. It doesn't matter which form of your Family Coat of Arms you chose; what matters is that you create a visual manifestation of what is important to your family. This becomes your personal Family Brand, or logo.

Your goal is to create symbolism for your design, something that the whole family will know the meaning of. Traditionally, in the coat of arms the shield that was used had a meaning. The colors represented values. The boarders, stripes, chevrons, and crosses, all had specific meanings of status, awards, or beliefs. Even the symbols of animals, plants, buildings, and patterns they used, all had specific meanings. Don't worry about the official meanings, make it meaningful to your family.

Let me give you an example of a Family Coat of Arms that some dear friends of ours from the United Kingdom developed.

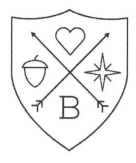

The simple Family Coat of Arms of our friends created.

My friend told me about what their Family Coat of Arms means to them, "*We came up with the motto, 'fortified in faith, love and righteousness'. We felt that these three things represented the kind of family we want to be - faithful, loving and righteous - so it's aspirational.*

*The acorn represents faith: how by exercising a little faith, great things can come about.*

*The heart represents love: we want our family to be knit together in love for each other and others.*

*The compass/star represents righteousness. The North star/lodestar provides direction and navigation. We want our family life to be guided and directed from above in a direct course. We want to follow the directions closely.*

*The shield and arrows refer to being 'fortified' - that if we truly embody these values, our family will be protected by and through them.*"

And of course, the letter "B" stands for their family name. Isn't that simply beautiful? You can tell what their family values are, and what is important to them. I hope that gives you a good idea of what a Family Coat of Arms can mean to your family.

If you're not sure where to begin, there are several ways you can create your Family Coat of Arms. The first, you can do it yourself – this is my recommendation because it will involve the whole family; Second, you can use an on-line app to help you design it (a simple internet search will give you several free do-it-yourself family crest makers); Third, if money weren't an issue, you could contract with a governing body, like the English College of Arms and pay them £5,750 (approximately $7,500 U.S. dollars) to design one for you.

Let me show you how to create your own Family Coat of Arms:

The first key to creating the coat of arms is to do it as a family. This will help everyone feel an ownership in the coat of arms and will make it more meaningful. It is an activity that your children will remember for years to come. I've included a Family Coat of Arms Template at the end of this chapter, to get you started.

The second key to creating your coat of arms is to have fun. It doesn't have to be perfect, but it needs to be your creation. Enjoy the experience. The process of creating your Family Coat of Arms gives you an opportunity to find out from all your family members what is important to them. Make the activity of creating it something enjoyable for everyone by keeping it lighthearted (especially with older children).

Third, don't worry about the official meanings of colors, shapes, or figures – do what is meaningful to your family. You can use the official symbolism if you want to, but only if it resonates with your family. It's easy to look up the meanings online. My recommendation is to use it as a guide if you're looking for ideas. Whatever you create, especially the meaning behind it, should have significance to you and your family.

Forth, incorporate your Core Family Values, a Family Mission Statement (if you have one), and anything else that is meaningful to your family, such as your family history, a trip, an experience, or even an inside family joke.

Fifth, create a Family Motto to accompany your Family Coat of Arms. It should be something short and meaningful. For example, in my family history, a famous person once told my fourth times great-grandfather, "Do right and obey counsel." That has become one of my family's mottos.

Finally, the sixth key is to get it printed. Put it somewhere where your family can see it. Refer to it often. Create your own brand management around your Family Coat of Arms to make it something important. Make it something special. Frame it, make it into family t-shirts, hats, mugs, cufflinks, broaches, or pins – anything to create enthusiasm for your Family Brand.

* * *

This is the end of the GATHER phase, and by now you should have identified some problem you want to work on together as a family to improve. The tools you have used so far have helped you as a parent to better understand what your family cares about. You should be able to see how everyone feels about the family from their individual point of view. You are now on your way to a successful family life with less stress and better communication.

Most exciting of all is that your family has now developed a road map of what's important to your family. By developing your Core Family Values you have created a belief system that will help you prioritize as you create solutions to your problems.

What I love most about the GATES™ framework is that it's not me telling you what you need to think or believe, or even defining what success means for your family. That's your job. You and your family know yourselves best and will be able to find solutions to improve your family.

> *"There are only two lasting bequests*
> *we can hope to give our children.*
> *One of these is roots, the other, wings."*
> *-Johann Wolfgang von Goethe*

# Family Coat of Arms Template.

## CREATE YOUR OWN PERSONAL FAMILY BRAND MANAGEMENT

# SECTION 2:

## *The GATES™ Framework - ASK*

**OBJECTIVES:**

**1.** Gain an in-depth knowledge of the area of improvement, focusing on identifying the root cause(s) of the problem.

**2.** Identify the value that can be created or improved to increase the quality of the situation.

**3.** Identify the waste that can be eliminated or reduced from the situation.

# CHAPTER 11

## The Power of Why?
## Finding the Purpose and the Root Cause

*Taking time to think, to ask why, can move your parenting from being reactionary to being proactive. Understand the purpose of things and you are half-way there. Find the root cause and you've solved the problem.*

In the first part of the GATES framework, you seek to understand the situation you want to change at a high-level. You *Gather* basic information about what the problem might be. Once you identify what needs to change, you *Ask* questions to get to the root cause. If you neglect this step, it's like applying ointment to an allergic rash without ever trying to identify what you are allergic to so that you can avoid it in the first place. In the ASK Phase you are now looking to identify the root cause(s) of what you want to improve, and you are beginning to develop solutions to make your family life easier.

### The Power of Why

The Power of Why is a simple yet very powerful business tool for getting to the root cause of an issue. Unfortunately, because its simplicity, it is often overlooked as the means of identifying the root cause. We ask "why" all the time so I'm sure you're scratching your head wondering *why* am I talking about using *why*, and how *why* can be used as a parenting tool?

The paradox is that children seem to be never ending with questions; yet as adults, we tend to stop asking questions. This is partly because we are conditioned and become afraid to ask a question that others might deem as a "dumb question."

Let me show you how asking *why* more often can help you (1) improve your understanding and clarity of purpose to *why* something needs to be done; (2) prioritize what you need to get done; (3) improve the quality or value of what you do, because when you understand the *why* behind things, your paradigms can shift and you can easily change your actions and behaviors; and it can help you to (4) understand your emotional states and the emotional states of others. When you are aware of your emotions you can better adjust your behavior to best fit the situation.

By **not** asking *why* more often, frankly, we are being intellectually lazy. By using this tool more in our lives, both at home and at work, we can understand the real reason something needs to get done. Understanding the purpose and motivation of things can positively influence how we do things and increase the value that we can provide.

When someone asks us to do something, we typically do it without questioning them to understand why they need it done. Later we find out that what they really wanted was something else done first, or you might have done what they asked, but they really wanted it done a little bit differently, or in a different order. Now to be fair, some of the failure was on *their* part for not explaining it well enough. However, that said, part of the blame is on *us*, because we assumed we understood what they wanted.

Of course, the word "assume" was the cause of the problem. You know what they say about those that assume? It makes an "a#@" out of "u" and "me."

You might find that by asking "*why?*" you will discover that the reason something is being done is not what you first thought it was. Understanding the *whys* behind something will affect the who, what, when, where, and how you do things. Greater effectiveness and efficiency result. Greater value can be added. Providing value is a fundamental of Lean, and asking *why* helps you get there.

Steps to using the Power of Why to improve your understanding of the purpose:

**1.** Understand the purpose. Ask *why* you are going to do a task or action? I'm not suggesting you question everything, but you can include your assumption of their purpose for clarification, when you restate what they want you to do. The key is to understand the purpose.

**2.** Determine if doing the activity will accomplish the *why* of doing it – the purpose. If not, don't do it. Instead offer a different solution that will support the purpose.

**3.** Accomplish the task by keeping your actions focused on the why(s) you identified. This might mean that you need to do it differently to accomplish the why, or you can add greater value when accomplishing the task because you now understand the purpose behind the request.

By really understanding the *why* behind what you are going to do, you can increase the value in how you do it. This becomes a win-win for everyone. By understanding the *why*, we understand the purpose, which will help us to adjust our behavior, so we can be more proactive instead of reactionary in what we do.

Let me give you an example of how this tool can be used at home. Once, I had a disagreement with my teenage son. I know, it's part and parcel of that dreaded state known as adolescence, but I was not amused by his attitude. I felt like grounding him forever, or at least until he moved out of the house – whichever came first. But, stopping for a second (Counting to Ten – another valuable tool) to break the anger and frustration I was feeling, I reflected, "*Why* am I doing this?"

Several answers came to mind. I love my son. I want to have him show me and the rest of the family the respect and love I feel we deserve. He needs to understand that his actions have consequences.

I was feeling reactive and I knew that would not benefit either of us. I wanted to be proactive and defuse the situation. I then asked myself several *why* questions to help me become more proactive with my parenting, "Why will the action of grounding him 'indefinitely' achieve my objectives?" "Why will he know that I love him by grounding him?" "Why will this consequence help my son to be more respectful?" "Why is he behaving this way in the first place?"

As I started asking why, I realized I had not given it enough thought. Anger, instead of reason, was writing the narrative. By stopping to ask *why*, I changed the dynamic of that situation. It could have developed into a reactionary conflict that would not have achieved the results I was looking for. Instead, through the love and concern of a parent, I gained control of the situation with a proactive thoughtful determination of what would benefit my son the most. This reflection allowed me to take a moment to think and consider an appropriate response which helped me be proactive in my parenting.

I removed myself from the situation and told him we would talk later. It is better to discuss consequences with your children after you have had an opportunity to calm down. After discussing the appropriate response with my wife and coming to an agreement (it is essential for parents to be on the same page, especially with discipline), we determined what would be an appropriate consequence of his actions.

We calmly explained this to him, being careful to keep our tone in a non-accusatory, concerned manner, and not raising our voices even when he raised his voice in protest. This is a crucial step to remember when dealing with children who are being argumentative. Be sure to remain calm and don't raise your voice, otherwise you are setting an example for your children that being argumentative is an appropriate behavior.

When dealing with our children, we need to model correct behavior. Arguments and disagreements can often be defused by keeping a calm and level tone when talking. It's hard to have a one-sided argument when one side is not participating – although children will often try.

Understandably, when emotional, this is not always possible. This is why you need to sometimes take a moment to gain control, to be proactive, before discussing a situation. A temporary break can work wonders in helping you regain control. Reactionary parenting rarely accomplishes what we want it to and can actually exacerbate the situation.

In this case with my son, I got part of the problem solved. But I also needed to understand where his disrespect was coming from by asking him why questions. In spending some time with him, almost 24 hours later, after things had cooled off, we had a heart-to-heart talk. Together we were able to discuss what had led to our earlier disagreement, and get to the root causes of the issue.

We need to stay close to our children and be the example they need us to be. Otherwise, the influence of pop culture and peer pressure can quickly overpower what we are trying to teach our children, if we are not careful.

Because I paused and asked *why*, I achieved my goals. I was able to be proactive and improve the relationship I have with my son. We got to a root cause of his behavior, while simultaneously teaching him the things he needs to know to be a better man. I could do this because he had opened up to me after we had both calmed down. All this from asking *why?* "*Why* will this action achieve the results I'm looking for?"

Taking time to be proactive will yield incredible results in your parenting. Pausing to think allows you to ask *why*, which will lead you to ways of identifying value that you can add to the situation. Start asking *why* more often, even to yourself, and you will be surprised to find that by understanding the reason behind things, you can find better, more efficient, or effective ways to do it. This is the Lean Way of parenting.

### The 5 Whys

Using *why* can not only help you better understand the purpose behind why something needs to be done so you can provide the value that is required, but it can also help you identify the root cause of a problem. This is another variation of the Why tool, and in business it is known as, "the 5 Whys." Frankly, I think that the person that came up with this tool probably had a five-year-old at home when they thought of it for work.

Just like how a small child is insatiably curious about their surroundings, the 5 Whys is used to get to the heart of the problem. The way you use it is similar to a five-year-old when they ask "Why?" You keep asking "why" until you get to the heart of an issue. Five might be the magic number for getting to the root cause, but keep in mind that it might take four times asking why or maybe even more. The point is, you ask *why* until you uncover what the real issue is. It's like peeling an onion, one layer at a time, until you come to the core.

The best way to see this in action is to demonstrate it. Here's a situation: Let's say that one of the rules at your house is for your kids to have their homework done by 8 p.m. Your kids know that they need to have their homework done by that time before they start getting ready to go to bed. Well, it's quickly approaching 8 p.m. and you find your child hasn't even started their homework.

One word of caution here before we start: try not to be judgmental when asking questions. As their parent you love them, and your tone of voice needs to reflect that love. If you want them to answer truthfully, the questions cannot contain accusations, frustrations, or irritations. You are asking the questions to help them, so make sure your voice reflects that love and concern.

[1] "Son, **why** haven't you started your homework, it's almost eight o'clock?"

Sheepishly he admits, "Well I guess I spent too much time watching TV." Most people stop here, DON'T!!! Now you may still ground them from watching TV for whatever time you feel is appropriate, but wait until you find out the root cause or causes before you start to discipline them. Rather, continue using the 5 Whys and let's see where it leads.

[2] "Son, **why** were you watching TV instead of doing your homework?"

"Well, I couldn't find the questions that the teacher assigned."

[3] "**Why** couldn't you find the questions?"

"Because the teacher put them on her website and I couldn't log on."

[4] "And can you help me understand, **why** weren't you able to log on?

"Well, because I couldn't remember my password." Ah-ha we got to the root of the problem in less than five *whys*, Right? Not quite, keep going.

[5] "**Why** couldn't you remember the password?"

"Well, I have the email from school that has my school password on it, but I forgot the password to my email account that you helped me set up, so I could log on."

[6] "**Why** didn't you ask me for help? I have it written down."

"I know. I tried to, but you were too busy and told me to leave you alone." UH-OH!!!

There you have it. If you stopped at the first *why*, we wouldn't have uncovered that there are other issues to solve. On the fourth and fifth *why*, we found out that the son needs to memorize his passwords, or at the very least have them written down.

Even though it's called the 5 Whys, don't stop with the fifth *why*. If you haven't gotten to the root cause of the situation, you keep asking questions until you uncover the root cause. Sometimes when you think you have gotten to the root cause of an issue, there is another root cause just below that one. By going a little deeper, on the sixth *why* in this scenario, you came to realize that *you* have something that *you* need to work on too. Such as not being dismissive when a family member needs something. Would you have ever come to this realization if you hadn't asked *why*? Perhaps not.

The goal of using the 5 Whys is to go beyond identifying the symptoms, to finding the root cause of an issue. This is a quick and simple tool. Please use it. But be aware, that by asking *why* all the time, you can come across sounding like a five-year-old, so soften the question with things like, "can you please help me understand *why* you did _____." "*Why* did you feel that _____ was the best course of action?" And, "When you did _____, what was your reason for why you did it?" There are plenty of variations to this question, so have fun coming up with your own find-out questions.

As in our example, you might find more than one root cause. That's okay. Finding them allows you to start working on ways to fix the issue so that it doesn't happen again, or it rarely happens. Either way, we are working on Continuous Family Improvement™ and we are teaching our children invaluable skills with how to be able to identify a problem and resolve it.

Also, keep in mind that sometimes the other person might give you two or three reasons behind a *why* question. When that happens, you create a branch for each answer, exploring each of their answers in turn with why until you get to the root cause of each of those reasons.

As parents, we want to provide a better life for our children. That means, we need to step up our game and improve ourselves. We need to be better at parenting. We need to understand *why* our children act the way they do. To do these things, we need to be willing to look at ourselves just as much as looking at our children. We need to be able to ask ourselves *why?* We need to be willing to get to the root causes of a problem and be willing to fix them, even if a root cause might point back at us.

The ASK Phase is important in making positive changes in the home. This one tool, the Power of Why, for finding out the purpose for doing something so we can provide the value that's needed, and the 5 Whys, for understanding the root cause(s), will transform the way you parent. Have fun, ask more questions of yourself and your children using *why*, and watch the magic happen within your family.

> *"He who has a why to live for*
> *can bear almost any how."*
> *- Friedrich Nietzsche*

JARED E. THATCHER

# CHAPTER 12

## The Personal Experience Wheel – Visualizing Your Personal Processes

*The ASK Phase is all about questioning your current state, and how to bridge the gap to your ideal future state. The Personal Experience Wheel will aid you in seeing what needs to change.*

The ASK Phase of the GATES™ framework is focused on two things. First, identifying the root cause of an issue, so you can fix the right things. Second, in this phase you are simultaneously developing solutions based on your inquiry to improve the problem. In Lean, one powerful tool that helps you accomplish both these objectives is the Value Stream Map. This tool is a visual method of identifying all the steps that go into a process.

While the Value Stream Map works well in a work setting, it is a bit too complicated to document the processes a family uses. I am therefore using a variation of the traditional Value Stream Map that conforms better to the needs of the family. This uncomplicated tool I am recommending is perfect for the whole family to use: The Personal Experience Wheel.

This tool is going to help you collect your thoughts, identify value and waste, and make all of this easily visible. This visual management tool will help you make purposeful steps towards continuous improvement of those things that need to be fixed. You will find that those improvements can be done with love and concern as your whole family works together to improve your family systems.

Let's examine a situation that happened in my home: my wife does not enjoy, or should I say *did* not enjoy the morning routine. It's easy to get yourself ready, but when you need to also make sure that the kids are ready, she felt some stress trying to make sure everyone was up, dressed, fed, out the door and ready to have a brilliant day.

Out of the whole routine of getting ready, there was one thing that irritated her more than anything else – waking up one of our sons. It wasn't so much the waking him up part, but rather every morning he would ask her a question that frustrated her. The first thing he said to her every morning was, "What time is it?" It became her personal pet peeve. There are clocks all over the house. She told him every morning to check the time for himself, yet every morning he still asked that same question, sometimes more than once.

To be fair, our son had no idea this was an issue. As we realized later, his motivation was to understand what time it was so that he knew how long he had to get ready before the bus left for school. For my wife, her desire was that he would embrace the habits of time management that would serve him well throughout his life, but every morning she had to intervene to make sure he was up and ready. This frustrated her.

A secondary frustration for her would be when the kids were running late and didn't have time to finish their breakfast. If breakfast really is the most important meal of the day, then she felt like they weren't going to have as good a day as they could have. That worried her.

One day, my wife mentioned to me how the morning routine of getting ready wasn't working and needed to change. She asked me if I had a business tool that could help her solve it. I had several, but the Personal Experience Wheel is the most visual and would work best in this kind of situation.

I ran her through the process, and within a matter of a few minutes she saw what she needed to do to solve it. She had written it down, and was now able to see exactly where the problem was. It became a visual management tool, where she could see and identify specific things that needed to change. She could make specific, meaningful improvements, without getting frustrated and stressed. The changes she made were done with love and concern for everyone. Best of all, it empowered our children to take on more responsibility for themselves.

The Personal Experience Wheel is a simple tool to use:

First, pick a recurring activity to map out. Recurring allows you to work on Continuous Family Improvement™ with some system or process. In this activity, I would like you to use your morning routine as the example, although you could just as easily do this with cooking, doing the dishes, laundry, or any other family process. On the Personal Experience Wheel Worksheet (found at the end of chapter) write down in the upper middle part of the circle where it says "experience," the type of experience you are documenting, in this case your morning routine.

Second, use the Five Whys to identify your motivation or purpose for the activity. Ask yourself "why?" until you identify what the true purpose of this activity is for you. What is your purpose or goal? Once you know what that is, write it down on the bottom half of the circle. Knowing this will be helpful later as you use that purpose to influence how you want to improve your problem areas.

Remember that the more impactful and moving that purpose statement is, the more motivation you will have to make the change.

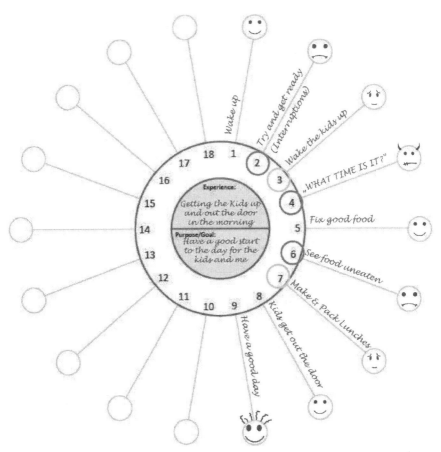

Next, identify each step in the order you take them during this activity you just identified. Starting with the first thing that happens, write that step on line number one. Continue around clockwise, with the next thing that occurs, writing it down on line number 2, and so forth.

Next, review each step to determine the value that is added at that point. In the circle at the end of each line, I want you to put a little emoji to represent how you feel at that step. The reason we do this is because it will help you to quickly identify any step that needs to be improved. If it is not providing you or others with value, we want to see that. Not every step in your process needs to make you feel happy or fulfilled, but it shouldn't make you feel like the poo emoji either.

This leads you to the second to last step: circle any number that you feel needs to be improved. My wife circled the steps that she felt she could eliminate in red, and ones she could improve in yellow as a visual management clue.

In Lean, we refer to these improvement areas as *Kaizen* Pain Points. *Kaizen* is the Japanese word for continuous improvement. Therefore, any step that needs to be improved is a pain point because it is not at its ideal state, thus they are called *Kaizen* Pain Points. Hopefully your Personal Experience Wheel will not have all the steps circled. If that's the case, and you have a lot of pain points, you might need to completely redesign the way you are doing your routine. Start over from scratch and redesign the process in the ideal future state.

If you think about it, how many of your reoccurring activities did you plan out in advance to make it a system that was both effective and efficient? What you are doing with this tool is mapping out in a visual way a system or routine, that was probably never thought through at the beginning before you started the process. This means you can evaluate everything you do and find ways to improve the value you contribute to almost any activity. You eliminate steps (waste) that don't add value, and you continuously improve your life by adjusting your routines and the steps within those routines.

Finally, you record all your *Kaizen* Pain Points on a Future State Solutions Worksheet, (from Chapter 8). List them under the current state side, and you can now ask yourself, what would be the ideal future state for this step? You might find that the step offers no real value, and as waste might be a step you could eliminate. Be sure to refer back to the second step where you wrote down your purpose statement, and think about how you could improve any of the *Kaizen* Pain Points, while keeping that purpose statement in mind. "What could I do differently that would help strengthen or achieve my purpose?"

After you've identified the ideal future state, try to think of at least three things that will help you bridge the gap between the current state and your ideal future state. Write down your ideas. These will form the bridge across the gap. Your ideas become your new pathway to a brighter reality.

So, let's go back to how my wife documented her Personal Experience Wheel. When it came to that question, "What time is it?" This is how she solved it:

My wife wrote down her frustration (*Kaizen* Pain Point) in the current state section of the Future State Solutions Worksheet. "This daily repeated question from my son is driving me crazy!" Keep in mind that her purpose for the morning routine was to have a good start to the day for the whole family.

I asked her, "What would the ideal state be for you in this step?"

She responded, "That it wouldn't be a step at all, because he could look for himself to see what time it was."

"Great, how can you eliminate this step out of your routine?" I asked. Instantly the idea hit her, "I need to make him responsible for getting himself up. Not only would he wake himself up by using his alarm clock, but he would also know the time. This will eliminate both my third and fourth steps from my daily routine!"

Wow! In just a few seconds, my wife eliminated two steps. Best of all her morning stress level decreased greatly. She didn't need to stress about waking him up or telling him every day what time it was, because she shifted the responsibility to him. And to think, this could have been resolved earlier.

Our son gladly took on this responsibility when it was given to him. He hadn't seen the need to do this before because his Mom always woke him up. Now both of them are happy. In fact, I'm happy to report that this son is now always the first one up and ready in the morning.

To illustrate how a Lean mindset will change your family, once our son overslept because of the snooze button. This inspired him to look for a way to continuously improve. On his own he bought a second alarm clock that he put away from his bed, which forced him to get up. He used this method until he got into a routine. Talk about continuous improvement.

Can you see the magic of going through the exercise and writing down the steps in your processes? When we write down each process step, they become visual. When it is visual, we see the problem from a different perspective, and the solution moves into focus. By analyzing our daily routines, we can find the waste in our systems that needs to be removed, and find ways to improve the quality of the value we provide. Through Continuous Family Improvement™ of processes, we can eliminate the little irritations that can build up over time.

I can't wait to hear how the Personal Experience Wheel and the other tools are working for you. Please share your successes and any questions you have in my free Facebook community page for this book at: fb.me/ParentingTheLeanWay

# The Personal Experience Wheel.

**A PROCESS MAP WHERE YOU SHOW HOW YOU FEEL ABOUT EACH STEP**

## DIRECTIONS

1. Pick an experience and record it in the middle.
2. Below that, document what the ideal purpose or goal should be.
3. Write the process steps of the experience on the lines radiating out (start with 1).
4. In the circles for each process step create an emoji for how you felt.
5. Circle any process step number that could be improved. (These are your Kaizen Pain Points)

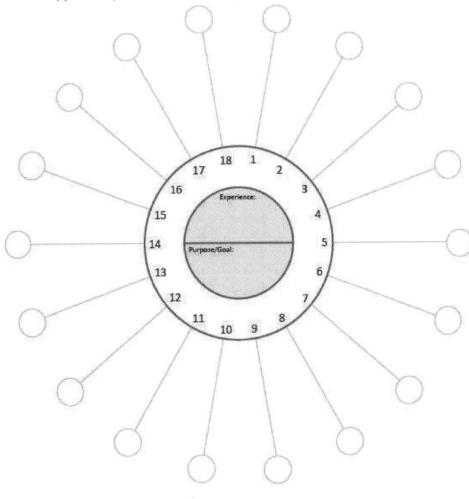

•◯• FamilyMBA

# CHAPTER 13

## Family Roles – Understanding the Needs of Others to Increase Value

*Part of getting to the root of a problem is understanding how the roles we have impact others. When we have this understanding, we can easily improve the value we provide.*

Many of the problems and frustrations we experience as parents are the result of our interactions with other people, and not from the inefficiencies of a process. While the Personal Experience Wheel works great for analyzing a process, its drawback is that it can't document personal interactions very well. The Customer Value Map is a tool which can help you visually document your interactions with others based on your role.

Just like a police officer, a firefighter, a soldier, a pilot, or a chef wear different hats to represent their different jobs and roles; each of us have distinct roles. Whether that role be a parent, spouse, child, sibling, friend, employee, boss, or any other role, how you behave and what you do in each role matters. For you to achieve your best results in your roles, you need to be open to take an introspective into the value you are providing.

As you examine your various roles using the Customer Value Map, improvement opportunities will become clear. You will identify in your roles more "customers" than you realized you had who are looking to you to provide them with value. You will craft and strengthen a clear purpose statement, which will help motivate you when you are in that role, and inspire you to enhance the value you provide. This tool will help you reduce the stress in your roles and make a more positive impact on those you are serving – especially in your role as a parent.

Now the Customer Value Map, is a simple exercise or tool that will allow you to gain a better insight into those you are serving in each of your roles. These insights can help you to know what others expect and value from you. With this understanding, your relationships with others will grow stronger as you demonstrate what you are willing to do for them.

Let's start by looking at the Customer Value Map, found at the end of this chapter. First, write down one of your roles on the top half of the center circle.

Next take a few moments to think about the purpose of that role. Your purpose statement is the reason you do this role – it's what gets you going. One way to think of the purpose statement of the role, is to think to yourself, "What would I most like to be remembered by others when they think about me in this role?" Put action words (verbs) into the purpose statement so that you feel inspired and motivated in this role. This is your mission statement for the role.

Next, you need to identify those you are serving in this role. At first glance, it might seem obvious when identifying these "customers" you are serving. I want you to think not just about those you are 1) serving right now, but also who you will either 2) be serving in the future, or 3) who will benefit secondhand from what you are doing in the role you are examining. I like to mark each "customer" as either direct (D), second-hand (S), or future (F) which helps me prioritize improvement actions I decide to take.

Let's take the role of parent, for example. Ideally you would list each child individually rather than simply putting children as your "customer." Don't think of "customer," as someone who pays you for what you do, but rather as the recipient(s) who benefits from your actions, or the value you provide to them.

Next, think of other customers who are secondhand customers benefiting from your role as a parent. This could be your children's friends, teachers, youth leaders, and coaches. Are you teaching your children, as their parent, the type of things that they need to know in order to be a true friend, to be respectful, attentive, and ready to interact with their teachers and coaches in a way that you and they would be proud of?

Who else are the "customer(s)" of your role as parent? Well, apart from your children, your spouse can benefit from your parenting. I know that there is no way my kids would be straight "A" students without my wife's parenting. Plus, she helps me in many other ways, including helping me give consistent messages to the kids.

Who else is a customer? Remember to think about who will benefit in the future from what I am doing in this role now. Any ideas?

Well, my children's future spouse, and my children's future kids (my grandkids) are, in one sense, people who will someday be "customers" of what I am doing today as a parent. Am I teaching my kids how to act as a parent, so that my future in-laws will be thankful for what I taught them? Will my future grandkids have the type of a parent I would hope they will have? That's on me to some degree in this role as a parent. I hope that I am living the type of example for my boys, so that they would want to be the same kind of husband and father in the future as I am now.

Now that you have identified the customers in your role, by first looking at those who directly benefit from what you do in that role; second, those who benefit secondhand from the value you are providing; and third, thinking of those who might benefit in the future from what you are doing now. Next, you should write down at least three things that you are *currently doing* in that role that will provide value to each of these "customers" that you have identified. What are you doing that creates value for them in your role?

Next, I want you to think about what you *could be doing* to provide value for each of these "customers." This might be something you do on an inconsistent basis that you should be doing all the time. Perhaps you realize that you aren't doing it now but you should, because it will add value. Think of this as an omission of what you could or should be doing.

Perhaps, you feel that your kids should be taking music lessons, but you can't afford them right now. Write it down anyway so that you don't forget your ideas. Don't preselect any idea out. Later, as you read through your answers you can start thinking of ways to accomplish things from this list, but for now, just write them down.

After you have written down the value you provide or would like to provide, take a moment to list anything you are currently doing that is a non-value-added activity, or waste. For example, nagging at the kids, or allowing screen time to be a substitute for family and social interactions. Or perhaps you are doing things for them that they are capable of doing for themselves (which is depriving them of the opportunities to learn and grow). As you make up this portion of the list, take a close look at what you wrote down and start to think of ways that you can eliminate or reduce what you are doing that is creating this waste.

As you begin to eliminate non-value-added activities, your stress levels will decrease. As you are serving people in your roles, you are going to find greater joy and happiness in your life. If you want to increase the love you feel towards someone, serve them. Concentrate on providing real value for them. Think of their needs, their situation and perspective from their point of view. As you do this, ill feelings will disappear, and your joy, happiness, and love will increase.

## Voice of the Customer Interviews

There is one additional tool I would like to provide you with that will be useful in the ASK Phase – the Voice of the Customer Interview. This is a very powerful tool for understanding the value we provide and the value others would like for us to provide to them.

This is not a formal interview or survey you are conducting, instead it should be conversational. Don't ask the questions in this manner, "from a scale of 1 – 10, ten being the best, how would you rate my performance with _____?" While in business a question like this might be appropriate, this type of question does not work in a home setting – I'm speaking from experience.

Just like the name suggests, a Voice of the Customer Interview is about hearing from your "customers" what they like and what they don't like about how you act in your roles. Keep the interview conversational. Ask questions like "Son, what do you think I do best as your Mom/Dad?" "What do you wish I did better for you as your

Mother/Father?" "If there is one thing I could do for you as your Mom/Dad, what would it be?" "What else? . . . and what else?"

If you show genuine interest and love as you conduct your Voice of the Customer Interview, you will find that your family and others will open up and tell you things that you can use to improve your performance in your role.

Now don't think for a second I'm suggesting that by asking your kids how to be a better parent, that I'm advocating you act on all of their suggestions. I'm not. If it were up to them, they would want us to allow them to stay up late into the night watching TV or playing video games. And forget about eating their vegetables, they would go straight for dessert. "Homework" wouldn't even be a word in their vocabulary. No, what I am suggesting is that you listen to them to understand the things that are of real value to them and to you, and then act accordingly.

Try to understand what they value. Something you thought was adding value, might not be as important to them as something else you do which you didn't think was very important, yet they value it very highly. For example, they might value you tucking them into bed every night, and giving them a hug and a kiss, more than playing a game with them on the weekend.

To truly add value in any role, you need to understand the needs of your "customer" or those you are serving. You might be shocked at what you find they truly value. By doing a Voice of the Customer Interview, you are going to improve your abilities in each role that you fill by providing those things that are of actual value to them.

Write down their answers. You'll then have a clearer vision of what you need to do in that role. You will see the gaps between their perspective of value and yours, so that you can adjust what you do accordingly. You now have the start of a plan on what things of value to provide to those you are serving, and a list of things you can work on eliminating that doesn't add value in your role.

Wow, that was a lot of info! But I hope that you see that it's worth the time to really understand the value you are providing in each role you fill – each hat you wear. Take the time to do these exercises for each of your roles. You will then have a road map for what to do and what not to do. This will help make your job easier in your role, increase your personal satisfaction, happiness, and reduce stress, while also improving the lives of those around you.

Can you imagine the impact you will have in your roles when you act with purpose? When your actions are focused on providing greater value? When those you are serving in each of your roles feel like you are going out of your way to do things just for them? There is power in thinking in terms of what the "customer" wants. There is power in providing value and eliminating waste. This is Parenting the Lean Way.

This really is nothing more than servant leadership. This is the essence of what parenthood is all about. This is how you want your children to be when they grow up. It starts with you. When you do things with purpose, and a focus on adding value, watch how your parenting improves and your family relationships mend.

Once you feel confident in defining and examining your roles, this is a great exercise to teach to your kids. Get them thinking about how they can add value in their roles. Get them thinking about what non-value-added activities they do that they can get rid of. Teach them how to continuously improve their lives.

Don't set an unrealistic expectation of perfection for your children, but teach them how to develop a mindset of Continuous Family Improvement™. Teach your children to think about what they can do differently today than they did yesterday. When you and they have adopted a continuous improvement mindset, cooperation improves, effort and drive increase, and life becomes easier.

This is what the ASK Phase is all about, getting to a deeper understanding of situations so you can develop a plan to improve it. Taking time to understand, so that you can act with love in proactive ways, instead of in the ignorance of a reactionary parenting style, is what makes this system different. Parenting the Lean Way is about seeking to understand before you act, so that your actions leave a positive impact on those you love.

They say that when planning any project, you want to spend the majority of your time planning the change and determining how to avoid any road blocks or resistance to change. You will therefore spend more time in the ASK Phase than in any of the other phases. How much time? Well, that depends on what you are trying to address. Don't worry about timing, worry instead about getting results.

At this point you should now have a road map for improvement from the information you have gathered and the self-reflection you have taken. By now you have identified the root causes of the issue you are trying to fix. You have converted your solutions into an improvement plan with your action steps listed in a SMART Goal format. You are also ready for any resistance to change that might occur. In the next phase, you will put your improvement plan into action.

*"Parents are the ultimate role models for children.*
*Every word, movement and action has an effect.*
*No other person or outside force has*
*a greater influence on a child than the parent."*
*- Bob Keeshan (Capt. Kangaroo)*

# ▌Customer Value Map – What is Your Role?
## VISUALLY DOCUMENTING WHAT YOU CAN DO TO STRENGTHEN YOUR RELATIONSHIPS

### DIRECTIONS

1. Pick one of your roles and write it in the upper part of the circle
2. Below that, put that role's purpose statement. Why does this role matter to you? What do you want to be remembered by others when they think of you in this role?
3. From the Identifying Your Roles Worksheet, list around the circle the Key People you serve in this role
4. Below each customer, write at least three things you do or should be doing to add value to them
5. BONUS: List three things you are doing that affect that individual or group that is creating waste

CUSTOMER(S):
**My Child's Friends (S)**
WHAT VALUE DO YOU PROVIDE?

1. Loyal & Forgiving
2. An Example w/ High Standards
3. Won't give in to peer presure

CUSTOMER(S):
**My Child (D)**
WHAT VALUE DO YOU PROVIDE?

1. Emotional & Financial Support
2. Provide Active Listening to them
3. Teach them how to solve life's problems

CUSTOMER(S):
**My Child's Teachers (S)**
WHAT VALUE DO YOU PROVIDE?

1. Inquisitive Zest for Learning
2. Contributes to Discussions
3. Goes beyond expectations

**ROLE:**
**Parent Extraordinaire**

**PURPOSE STATEMENT:**
To raise self-sufficient, charitablechildren prepared for life

CUSTOMER(S):
**Child's Future Spouse(F)**
WHAT VALUE DO YOU PROVIDE?

1. How to treat their spouse
2. How to be a great listener
3. How to care for a family

CUSTOMER(S):
**My Child's Coach (S)**
WHAT VALUE DO YOU PROVIDE?

1. Demonstrates Sportsmanship
2. Follows Directions & Works Hard
3. Demonstrates Leadership & Support

CUSTOMER(S):
**My Future Grandkids(F)**
WHAT VALUE DO YOU PROVIDE?

1. To be a better parent than me
2. Unselfishly gives of their time
3. Teach them how to love life

CUSTOMER(S):
**Child's Future Boss (F)**
WHAT VALUE DO YOU PROVIDE?

1. Taught a Work Ethic
2. Knows how to solve problems
3. Able to provide value

CUSTOMER(S):
**Child's Future In-Laws (F)**
WHAT VALUE DO YOU PROVIDE?

1. Well mannered
2. Provides for spouse and kids
3. Understanding of their relationship

### WHAT WASTE COULD YOU ELIMINATE?

1. Dismissive after returning from work
2. Rescuing them by reminding/nagging
3. Overly critical

Customer Type Key:
(D) Direct
(S) Second-hand
(F) Future

•○• FamilyMBA

# ▐ Customer Value Map – What is Your Role?

VISUALLY DOCUMENTING WHAT YOU CAN DO TO STRENGTHEN YOUR RELATIONSHIPS

## DIRECTIONS

1. Pick one of your roles and write it in the upper part of the circle
2. Below that, put that role's purpose statement. Why does this role matter to you? What do you want to be remembered by others when they think of you in this role?
3. From the Identifying Your Roles Worksheet, list around the circle the Key People you serve in this role
4. Below each customer, write at least three things you do or should be doing to add value to them
5. BONUS: List three things you are doing that affect that individual or group that is creating waste

CUSTOMER(S): _____

WHAT VALUE DO YOU PROVIDE? _____

1.
2.
3.

CUSTOMER(S): _____

WHAT VALUE DO YOU PROVIDE? _____

1.
2.
3.

CUSTOMER(S): _____

WHAT VALUE DO YOU PROVIDE? _____

1.
2.
3.

ROLE:

PURPOSE STATEMENT:

CUSTOMER(S): _____

WHAT VALUE DO YOU PROVIDE? _____

1.
2.
3.

CUSTOMER(S): _____

WHAT VALUE DO YOU PROVIDE? _____

1.
2.
3.

CUSTOMER(S): _____

WHAT VALUE DO YOU PROVIDE? _____

1.
2.
3.

CUSTOMER(S): _____

WHAT VALUE DO YOU PROVIDE? _____

1.
2.
3.

CUSTOMER(S): _____

WHAT VALUE DO YOU PROVIDE? _____

1.
2.
3.

WHAT WASTE COULD YOU ELIMINATE?

1.
2.
3.

| Customer Type Key: |
| --- |
| (D) Direct |
| (S) Second-hand |
| (F) Future |

•◯• FamilyMBA

# SECTION 2:

## *The GATES™ Framework - TINKER*

**OBJECTIVES:**

**1.** Prioritize the solutions you developed and get commitment and support from each family member to hold each other accountable.

**2.** Work on implementing the solutions to your root cause(s) that you have identified.

**3.** Anticipate possible unintended consequences and resistance to change and adapt your improvement plan if necessary.

# CHAPTER 14

## Prioritizing and Limiting Your Work in Progress – Stay Focused and Avoid Multi-Tasking

*Limiting Work in Progress is a simple tool, but one that will greatly improve your time management skills (effectiveness) and help you become more efficient too. Best of all, concentrating on one thing at a time is a simple way to reduce the stress you feel.*

I n the previous two phases of the GATES™ framework, you have completed certain objectives necessary for solving issues you want to fix in your family. In the GATHER Phase, as a family, you have identified an area you want to improve. You also developed the core values that are important to your family. These values will guide you as you prioritize the things you want to improve.

In the ASK Phase, you sought both to understand the problem and to identify its root causes. These insights you gained, along with your future state vision of what your improvement would look like, helped you develop solutions. A basic understanding of people's resistance to change should have given you some ideas on how to make sure your improvement plans will be a success.

Now is the phase where the action is really going to start taking place. You get to act and see which solutions work and which do not. This is the TINKER Phase – an opportunity to try your solutions. Just like when you played with Tinker Toys® as a kid, there was no wrong way to build your creation. The same is true as you implement your solutions. That said, there are two things to keep in mind as your family tries out the solutions: prioritization and limiting Work in Progress.

You may have come up with several ideas for how to resolve or improve your family's issue and you may be wondering which one you should work on first? I have two suggestions. First, prioritize your ideas by which one will have the greatest positive impact towards the realization of your goal. Work on improving these action steps in that order of importance.

Second, you also want to get the family excited about making the change, so a quick-win would be fantastic. If you have any ideas that you can implement immediately, or in a relatively short period of time, have those ready to use to motivate the family. The whole family can get excited about seeing movement toward your goal, so you might want to use these quick-wins at both the beginning of this phase and at a point in time where resolve to complete the improvement is waning.

I've said it before, and it's important enough to have a short chapter on it, be sure to limit your Work in Progress! If you try too many things at once, you will become overwhelmed and it will take longer to accomplish your goals – if you even achieve them at all. There is a risk that if you overload your family or yourself with too many action steps, you will feel overwhelmed and you will never complete your improvement plan.

In a Lean workplace, we typically do not work on any more than three items at the same time. Ideally, one at a time works best, but this is not always practical at work. In your home, you will find that your children will perform best when you are working on only one idea or action step at a time.

During your Family Board meeting, be sure to stress the importance of everyone working on accomplishing the current solution idea to improve the area your family is working on. By daily reviewing the solution step you are trying to implement, you will get cooperation and unity to solve your improvement opportunity. Be sure to find out from all the people involved in that solution step, how it is going, what they are focused on achieving next, and if they need any help. This simple formula will help your family make remarkable improvements and strengthen your family relationships.

I want all of you to teach a valuable lesson to your children which is that drive, determination, and focus will get them further in life than trying to multi-task their way to success. Limiting your Work in Progress will help everyone stay focused on achieving the value and results you want.

### The Multi-Tasking Myth Busting Challenge

To prove this point, I am going to provide you with a fun exercise you can do with your family to show them how much more efficient it is to work on one thing at a time rather than trying to multi-task. The Multitasking Challenge Worksheet at the end of this chapter will help you understand this point better. You'll need to have a stop watch to time how well you do in the following two challenges.

The first challenge will be to time yourself, or your children, and see how fast you are able to multi-task. To do this, write in the first column in the first row the number one. In the second column write the Roman numeral for the number one "i". In the last column write the first letter of the alphabet "a." Then go back to the first column in the second row and write the number two, then write the Roman numeral for two "ii" in the second column, and then the second letter in the alphabet "b" in the last column. Repeat this process all the way to 10. How long did that take you? Write down your time.

The next challenge is about focusing on one task at a time. Do this by writing all the numbers between 1 and 10 in the first column, then move to the next column and write all the Roman numerals between one "i" and ten "x", and finally, write all the letters of the alphabet sequentially between "a" and "j." You are going to be working by single tasks or one column at a time. How long did this take you?

Depending on how well you know your Roman numerals, you completed the single task in half the time to about a third of the time faster than when you were trying to multi-task. This clearly shows that by limiting our Work in Progress, by staying focused on one task at a time (ideally our highest priority task first), we can complete our tasks faster. Therefore, avoid multi-tasking. You want to limit the Work in Progress (the "Doing" section) to only a couple of items at a time.

While this might seem counter intuitive to have more than one task in the "Doing" section, it works. For example, while you're waiting for the laundry to finish, or for someone to call you back with some information, you can be working on another task. By limiting your work in progress, you are still essentially focusing on doing one task at a time. Focus allows you to get more done, faster. Prioritize your most important tasks first, and you will be more productive in what you do. What a wonderful time management lesson to teach your family.

# Multi-Tasking Myth Busting Worksheet.
## GET A STOP WATCH, AND TAKE THE CHALLENGE

### Multi-Tasking Three Different Tasks at the Same Time

1-10          I-X          A-J

1st →
2nd →
3rd →
4th →
5th →
6th →
7th →
8th →
9th →
10th →

TIME: _____

### Focusing on One Task at a Time

↓1st            ↓2nd            ↓3rd
1-10          I-X          A-J

TIME: _____

WHAT DID YOU LEARN FROM THIS CHALLENGE?

FamilyMBA

# CHAPTER 15

## How to Run a Mini Sprint™ – Focusing on the Task at Hand

*The Mini Sprint™ is a practical tool that makes work fun, teaches the family about planning, prioritizing, organizing, problem solving, time management, and Continuous Family Improvement™. Perfect to TINKER around with possible solutions.*

A typical solution that many families decide to address first in the TINKER Phase is cleaning the home. When you have a clean and organized home, your family members can take pride and ownership in it. Lean has a methodology and tools specifically for cleaning a work space known as 5S. It received that name because the five phases of this cleaning methodology all start with the letter S in Japanese. While 5S is a nice system for cleaning, organizing, and continuing to keep an area clean, I want to introduce you to an Agile tool that is simple to learn and perfect for motivating the whole family to clean the house.

I initially borrowed this tool from IT software development to help motivate the family to clean the house. It has other applications as well, including my son now using it to manage his homework. I call this tool the Mini Sprint™. The term Sprint comes from the IT world in business where the Agile methodology developed from Lean. In Agile they refer to a Sprint as a predefined period of time to accomplish certain tasks. The idea behind a Sprint is like a race – you sprint to the end. You work hard until you reach the goal.

This is a way to motivate kids and parents to do a quick clean and pick-up – a sprint cleaning. The Mini Sprint™ is basically a souped-up chore chart that is going to help you get more done, faster than you though possible, with increased quality in what you do. The great thing is that this can also be used for doing homework and other projects as well. This is both a time management tool as well as an organizational tool. It will help teach your children cooperation, taking pride in their work, and leadership skills, as they work to achieve the tasks they have been assigned. Let's begin by explaining what a Mini Sprint™ is all about.

In Agile, a Sprint typically lasts between a week to three weeks. While this length of time might be perfect in business for software development, it would never motivate any family member to clean the house over that same period. When you think of a sprint, you think of a race where one runs as fast as they can until they reach the finish line. This is not a long-distance marathon where you pace yourself.

We want to use the Mini Sprint™ in a similar way. A brief period of time where you work as hard as you can, as quickly as you can, to accomplish a set of tasks. I recommend no more than two hours for a family. You sprint from task to task until you have completed all the tasks, or your time is up. When you treat this like a race to see how much you can get done within the sprint "time frame," you make this a game. It will be a fun activity that your family will enjoy, although maybe not at first.

The first step is to set a Time Box and then stick to it. A Time Box is a predefined time, where once the time is up, you stop. You will want to keep this realistically aggressive, meaning that if you think the tasks will take an hour and forty-five minutes to complete, you shave off fifteen minutes and make it an hour and a half.

This does two things. First, it forces you to stay on track because you know you don't have time to waste. Second, it causes your mind to think of innovative solutions to become more efficient and effective with the tasks you are doing, simply because you know that you have less time to complete them.

What happens if you don't finish in the time frame you Time Boxed out?

Stop anyway. Be sure to keep the trust of your family. If you said an hour, then it's an hour. I'll explain a few strategies in a minute, but don't extend the time. What you might find is that the kids will actually beg you for more time, so they can finish their tasks. Wouldn't that be a switch?

And it does happen! It becomes an exercise in reversed psychology, because you are telling them that there won't be any more time. This might not happen right away, but once they see that you are serious about the Time Box, you will see a change in both how fast they do tasks and how much they want to complete everything on their list.

You're probably thinking, "What if the time is up, but we have not finished cleaning the house, and we have company coming this evening?" I feel your concern, and I've been there. But again, you need to establish trust with your kids. More importantly, as a parent, you need to stop rescuing your kids. It doesn't do your children any favors. They need to learn about natural consequences.

Of course, if your kids are in immediate physical danger – rescue them. Apart from that, parents need to learn to stop rescuing their children and now is the perfect time to start. This means that if the house still needs work and all of you working together didn't finish it in time – and I'm willing to bet it's because the kids were taking their own sweet time and didn't finish their tasks – then you need to stop at the end of the Time Box and that's it. Let them see what happens when the job doesn't get done.

You see, our kids test us on many fronts. Are you as the parent, going to stick to the Time Box? If they didn't finish, are you, the parent, going to finish cleaning for them so that you don't feel embarrassed when the guests arrive? And/or, they will complain about doing this, just to see if you really believe in using this tool and will follow through, or if you will stop when they make it difficult for you. Trust me, your kids will test you.

After setting up the Time Box, the second thing you need to do is to gather everyone who will be participating together to have a Kick-off Meeting. By "meeting" I'm talking about a few minutes to plan the activities, so the work will go faster. This is where you explain the purpose of the Mini Sprint™ For example: cleaning the house, or cleaning the bedrooms, or doing yard work.

Once the purpose is established, solicit from the kids the tasks which they feel are essential for completing that purpose. Now to speed things up, I'm sure that you have already written down some tasks on sticky notes, but leave some obvious ones for the kids to come up with. This helps to get their buy-in for the jobs to be done. Where appropriate, you can write the task on the sticky note either as a picture (visual management) for the younger kids or in a story format.

Don't forget that once you have created a task, the final step is to get agreement as to what the Definition of Done is for the task. This will set the person up for success by knowing exactly what they need to do, *and* help avoid arguments later. To learn more about the Definition of Done, see Chapter 17.

Next, take a minute and get agreement from the kids about how long each task will take. By getting agreement on how long the tasks will take, you will be able to fairly divide up the jobs so that everyone has a similar amount of work load to do. This is important, so you can do the next part of the Kick-off Meeting, assigning tasks.

Once you know how long the tasks will take, divide up the tasks. Ideally, you have the children choose which tasks they would like to complete. However, knowing how children can be, this might lead to fighting, so you might want to start by dividing up most of the tasks yourself, and then try having them choose one additional task to reach the amount of time needed to keep it within the Time Box. If you have established the Time Box in a realistically aggressive time frame, then the tasks should take about the same amount of time, or just over the amount of time set.

You might find that after you figure out how much time all the tasks will take, adjusting the Time Box before you start might be prudent. But if this is the case, it is best to get agreement from everyone, rather than making a dictatorial proclamation. Again, it goes back to trust. If you set the Time Box before the meeting and now you are changing it, albeit for a good reason, this can still erode trust. Make sure everyone agrees or at least that there is a consensus. If you have a strong enough purpose statement, it shouldn't be a problem, because your family will want to successfully complete the purpose.

A better way to do it would be to issue a challenge to the kids, "Now that we know how long this should take, do you still think we can achieve our purpose of (and restate the purpose of the Mini Sprint™)? Do we want to increase the time a little bit, or do you think we can sprint really hard to get all of these tasks done in the time frame we have set?" You might be surprised to find they ask for more time, or they might want to take the challenge to try and get it done in the time already allocated.

Once you have the Kick-off Meeting (and this should be kept very short, 10 minutes maximum), and everyone knows why they are doing the Mini Sprint™; what tasks they are going to do; what the

Definition of Done is for each task; how long the tasks will take, who is doing which task; and the Time Box has been agreed to – now is the time to start the Mini Sprint™. Look at the clock and let everyone know what time you are stopping. Remember to make it a game, so start the count down, "READY, SET, GO!" You are now Time Blocking. Don't let anything else distract you, stay on task, minimize your WIP (Work in Progress). Move things across your Mini Sprint™ Kanban Board from "To Do" to "Doing" to "Done."

Do a countdown as you are Time Blocking. Let everyone know at the half-way point and with ten minutes, five minutes, and one-minute remaining, 30 seconds, and TIME! This countdown will both help everyone realize how much time is left, but also inspire everyone to work a little faster.

Now for the final step: The Mini Sprint™ Retrospective Meeting. This is another short 10-15 minute meeting at the end. Everyone comes together to update the Kanban Board with their final results (if you need a refresher of a Kanban Board see Chapter 5).

Because it is a visual management board, you can see who finished, who nearly finished, and who didn't do very well. Once the Mini Sprint™ board is updated, you need to make this a positive experience. Your kids are probably going to test you the first few times. Stick with it and you will see positive changes. Congratulate them sincerely for what they did get accomplished. And I mean keep it sincere. No passive-aggressive compliments. You want everyone to feel good about what they accomplished, even if it wasn't a lot.

Next, take the lead by reporting to the family how your tasks went. Tell everyone what went well, especially if you did something innovative to save time. Share those successes so that everyone can learn from them in the future.

Let your family know if you didn't complete a task. Teach them it is important to take ownership for your mistakes. If you didn't complete a task, explain what prevented you from completing it. Set an example for your kids by not making excuses or placing blame. Instead, state facts, be willing to say you didn't complete everything, and present a plan on how to solve it next time. Let everyone know what you will do next time to be able to complete the task.

Did you need a little more time? Do you need to have the cleaning supplies ready to go? Could you not find the cleaning supplies? Present a solution. Don't just talk about your plan to do better, do it. And then later let your family know you did it. For example, next time you will create a special space for the cleaning supplies, so you don't waste time finding them.

"Hey everyone, I stopped by the store today and picked up containers to hold all of our cleaning supplies and you can find them under the bathroom and kitchen sinks." You need to set the example, which is the reason you go first, to show your family how to report back. Again, the order is:

- Here is what I accomplished.
- Here is what went well and why.
- Here is what didn't go well and how I plan on solving it next time.

Have each family member go through the exercise of sharing with the whole family those three things.

This Retrospective Meeting is going to become an important step in your family's effort for Continuous Family Improvement™. It will help teach them problem-solving skills. It will help them estimate their time usage better. As you do more and more Mini Sprints™, they will get better and better at estimating how long it will take. These are the basics of the Mini Sprint™.

The Mini Sprint™ is simple, but as you use this format, you need to stick with it. You will most likely be met with some resistance in the beginning, but over time you will find that the kids look forward to doing a Mini Sprint™. In fact, they might even begin to create their own Mini Sprint™ boards. Don't believe it? It will happen. But you need to remain positive. Don't put anyone down for not finishing. And keep your word when Time Blocking.

If you want to take the Mini Sprint™ to the next level, create a point system. Each task has points associated with it once the task is completed. If your kids work together in cooperation on a task, they get a certain amount of points. At the end of the Mini Sprint™, during the Retrospective Meeting, tally up the points for each person. You need to have a list of rewards in advance, so they know what they are working toward, but this can be an effective way to motivate them into action.

Another option would be to have small prizes ready to reward task completion at the Retrospective meeting. This could be anything from a trip to the park, a hike, a small treat, etc. Give the prizes for things they did: teamwork, first one done, attention to detail, most innovative idea for cleaning, most focused on completing the task, etc. You can come up with dozens of things to reward them for, with each one teaching them a valuable lesson.

I hope that gives you a couple of ideas. You know your kids best, so with a little bit of effort beforehand on your part, you can make your Mini Sprint™ a fun activity that they will look forward to doing. They are learning about time management, problem solving, and team work, while also developing a work ethic at the same time without them even realizing it.

Best of all, after a while, you will find your kids doing their own Mini Sprint™ for cleaning their room or doing their homework. Don't believe me? Well, one of my sons uses it every day to organize his homework and for what he needs to study for a test. He says that he can't imagine not having this tool in *his* tool belt. If done right, your kids will make this one of their tools, without you forcing it on them, because it works!

Remember that the TINKER Phase is all about experimenting and trying to improve whatever you are working on. The beauty of the Mini Sprint™ is that it can be used for a quick clean, or even for a longer improvement project. If you are doing a longer project, instead of running the Mini Sprint™ for an hour or two, you would run it for a week at a time and incorporate it into your Family Board.

Getting your kids to learn to visually see tasks will help them in completing their work. Limiting their Work in Progress will help them improve their focus. Reviewing what went well and what needs to improve is what the Sprint Retrospective is about. Tinkering around looking for solutions will help your family embrace Continuous Family Improvement™.

# THE MINI SPRINT™ STEPS:

- Establish a Time Box (and stick to it!)
- Kick-Off Meeting
  - Announce the Purpose of the Mini Sprint™
  - Create Tasks (use pictures for younger kids)
  - Establish a Definition of Done (See Chapter 17)
  - Estimate Time for Tasks (helps to prioritize)
  - Assign or Choose Tasks
  - Add up Time of Tasks Once Chosen
  - Re-evaluate the Time Box if Necessary
  - Start the Mini Sprint™ with a Count Down
- Give a Count Down to the End of the Time Box
- Stop the Tasks and Return to the Board
- Mini Sprint™ Retrospective Meeting
  - Update the Mini Sprint™ Kanban Board (To Do/Doing/Done)
  - Report Out to Everyone:
    - What You Did
    - What Went Well and Why
    - What Didn't Go Well & How You Will Improve it Next Time

# SECTION 2:

## *The GATES™ Framework - EXPERIMENT*

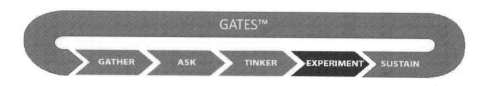

## OBJECTIVES:

**1.** Track your improvements visually through KPIs (Key Performance Indicators).

**2.** Hold regular meaningful communication to increase cooperation and implement successful improvements

**3.** Keep each other accountable for actions.

# CHAPTER 16

## Key Performance Indicators (KPIs) – Holding Each Other Accountable

*The EXPERIMENT Phase will help you test your solutions. Don't let the solving of a problem overshadow the love needed by the individual, in other words, numbers are good, but people are more important.*

A friend of mine from work was able to reduce his electricity bill using a very simple business tool. He tracked the performance of his family in reducing their expenses by comparing their current usage with the previous year. With the electric bill, this was an easy thing to do. The bill includes the previous month's usage, so you can track how well you are doing at reducing the cost of your electricity usage. My friend would put the bill up on his Family Board so that all the kids could see what their goal was and how well they had done in the previous month. Visual management made achieving their goal a reality.

Once he involved his kids, he no longer had to remind them to turn off the lights. They took ownership for achieving the results. They started to remind him. How is this possible? He arranged with them that whatever amount of money they saved over the previous year, he would split the savings with them. They got paid based on the success of their effort.

In the business world, we refer to the tracking of performance as a Key Performance Indicator or a KPI. From here on out, I will be referring to the tracking and graphing of your performance as KPIs. As you use them in your home, you will feel the impact of KPIs to help you to achieve your family goals and improve your personal development goals, because they create accountability.

The KPI is similar to a star chart used by teachers to track the progress of their students. Where the star chart tracks events and motivates, a KPI can also do that and so much more.

The KPI can compare and contrast current performance with past performance or between individuals, measure both quantitative and qualitative information, leading and lagging indicators, and financial data. If all this seems complicated, it's not. KPIs are a simple tool to make activities visual.

Where managers, executives, and investors use KPIs to see how well a company and employees are doing, parents can likewise use KPIs to help monitor progress at home. KPIs are used to help measure predefined activities and performance necessary to show the progress being made towards goals. There is after all a famous business maxim that says, "You can't change what you don't measure."

KPIs in the home are an excellent tool to affect personal change and achieve your goals. A Key Performance Indicator helps ensure success in your endeavors due to several factors:

First, it creates accountability. When you know that you are being watched and assessed, your actions change because of your accountability to others. You want to look good when you know others are watching.

Second, it provides a constant reminder of your goals. Every time you update your KPIs you are constantly referring to your goals. By tracking your progress, you can't help but keep your goals always at the top of your mind.

Third, it has a motivating effect. You want to see your KPIs reflect positive results because you and others are watching to see how you do. This tends to help motivate you to act toward the outcomes you are trying to achieve.

Fourth, results are made visible. KPIs are a form of visual management, meaning that you can quickly see whether or not you are making progress towards your goal.

Fifth, it creates objectivity. When creating a baseline, you can benefit from the "observer effect." When you are focused on gathering information, it creates a natural barrier between you and those you are observing. You can distance yourself from what's going on and not react in your typical manner, because you have taken on the role of an observer. It becomes about watching and recording behavior, and not engaging in what you are observing.

The observer is just that, the observer, not the participant. As the observer, you do not need to get emotional and engage. To quote Sergeant Friday from the old TV show Dragnet, "Just the facts Ma'am." Which leads us to our final factor of the successes of KPIs.

Sixth, a KPI allows you to stay calm when discussing the results. Why? Because KPIs are based on measurements, which form facts. When discussing the changing of a behavior, you don't need to get emotional, you can stay calm and refer them to the measurements, the facts. "I'm sorry that your brother hit you twice, you still hit him five times, didn't you?" Don't get sucked into arguing. The facts are there, and they speak for themselves. You know, it's liberating to be objective, in control, and proactive, instead of emotional and reactive. KPIs give you that ability. They help reduce stress. Try it, you'll see.

KPIs will help your family improve and change behaviors. If anyone doesn't want to track a KPI, they are basically saying that they don't want to be held accountable for their actions. It is important, therefore, to get everyone on board to make your family KPIs successful.

Don't let the solving of a problem overshadow the love needed by the individual. Use KPIs with your family out of love and concern, not as a cold calculating tool to try and change behavior. If everyone is on board with trying it, KPIs can be a powerful tool. If they are fighting it, it is unlikely to yield any lasting results. Don't forget that people are more important than the numbers.

* * *

Remember the Current State/Future State Focus Group workshop from Chapter 6? One of the things I asked you to do was to write down both the good and the bad things that came out of those workshops. Go back to your Future State Solutions Worksheet. Is there a common thread that the family universally agrees on that needs to change in your family? Figure out how to quantify that improvement and then create a KPI around it. Begin to measure your progress and keep updating it on a regular basis.

Let me give you an example of how this worked with a family from one of my workshops:

After completing the Family Focus Group workshop, everyone in this family mentioned that there was too much yelling in their house. The kids would yell at each other for some minor infraction, which in turn got their mother to yell at them. Then the father would come home and yell at everyone for yelling. They all wanted to live in a home where they spoke pleasantly to one another, yet they weren't sure how to get there, because their "best" efforts didn't seem to be making a difference.

I explained to the families in the workshop that they needed a tool that would help them see their progress towards their goal while at the same time create accountability for everyone involved. That tool is a KPI. For this family, they were going to use a KPI to measure how much they yelled and to track their progress, so they could reduce and eliminate the need to yell.

After providing them some examples of KPIs, this family created a simple KPI that consisted of a grid on a 3x5 note card. In the rows it had everyone's name, and in the columns, the days of the week. With the far-right hand column being used to total up the amount of times they yelled during the week.

I had them define the scope of what they would measure, and I gave some ideas to their family on how they could track their yelling. What they came up with was that the person yelling would get a tick mark when they would yell. Not for every word or sentence, but one mark would suffice. If they are still carrying on after a minute, they would get another tick mark for each additional minute of their rant. Anyone could put down a tick mark on the KPI sheet.

They were all responsible for making sure that any yelling got captured, even if that meant self-reporting. Now watch what happens, because your kids are going to love this as much as their kids did. The parents said that they had never seen their kids move so fast to run up to the Family Board to put a tally mark on the KPI. You know, it's rather hard to yell at someone, because as soon as they start to yell, the other person disappears to put a mark on the KPI.

According to the parents by the end of the first week, it dawned on everyone that they were creating a baseline and they had better watch the tone and volume of their voice. Once they had their first week's baseline of how much each of them yelled, they determined what their goal should be for the next week. They agreed to try and reduce it by at least half. Every week they would half that previous week's amount again and so on until they weren't yelling at each other. It took them about six weeks to get to the point where no one yelled more than one or two times during the week.

Some weeks they made it, some weeks they didn't. The point is, they were working on it. That's what Continuous Family Improvement™ is all about. It's not about being perfect, but about making an honest effort to be better. They tracked it for a few more weeks after they felt like they had reached their goal. Then they decided to suspend the KPI, at which time they created another KPI to work on something else. Just think of how much you and your family could improve if you were always working on one or two KPIs.

About a year-and-a-half later, during a Family Board Meeting, this family decided to bring back the KPI to help them with the yelling that had begun to resurface. This time, they said it took them only a week-and-a-half to change their behavior. Because of the visual management of the KPI, the daily Family Board Meetings, and the personal accountability that it created, they were able to quickly self-correct their behavior. Plus, they knew it was possible to change, because they had already done it.

Be aware that with KPIs you might also have people try and sabotage your efforts. Case in point, on the second week this father was heading into the last day without having yelled all week. His kids conspired to push his buttons so that he would yell at them, so that they could mark him down for yelling. He said, "Those little rascals entrapped me, and they got their tick mark. It was later that I learned they had done that on purpose."

The great thing about KPIs is that they really help you to make a difference in achieving your goals quicker. Once your kids see the success they have with improving the home, they will come to love KPIs and use them on their own.

A while ago, we were trying to get our daughter to put away her toys after playing with them. Just when we thought she had learned, she would backslide. It was a bit of a struggle. In our family meeting, when our daughter was reviewing her goal to put away her toys, she mentioned that she was having a tough time remembering to do it. Our son offered her a suggestion. "Why don't you create a KPI, you could track when you put your toys away? I'll bet it would help you remember to do it. Plus, I know you would love putting princess or animal stickers on it."

I was amazed that he thought of it before we did. I told him that he had a great idea and asked if he would develop a KPI for his sister to keep track of her progress. Can you imagine how that made him feel? Not only had he come up with a great idea, but he was made responsible for the design of the KPI chart for his sister to use.

Every chance you can find the opportunity, allow your children to contribute to the family. It provides them with a sense of pride. Give them a chance to lead and be responsible for something. KPIs provide that opportunity to our children.

After the meeting, our son went to the computer to design and print a weekly chart for his sister. He helped her put it on the wall of her bedroom and explained to her that she could put a sticker on her chart every time she put away her toys. My wife bought her some stickers and our daughter got excited about putting them on her clean-up KPI chart every day she put her toys away.

Within two weeks, she was putting the toys away without being reminded. She continued to use her KPI chart for another two or three months because she loved it so much. When she finally stopped using it, she had formed a habit and didn't have to be reminded anymore.

In terms of tracking a KPI, you will probably notice two trends. The first is that a few days after starting a new KPI, the behavior might get worse. They might challenge using the KPI. This is natural for your kids to test your resolve. But if they contributed to developing the KPI, they will get on board and work toward achieving their goal, especially when they see you are committed to it as well.

The second trend is known as spontaneous recovery, which will usually appear after a couple of weeks of tracking a KPI and refers to the reappearance of the behavior you are trying to get rid of after a brief period where it appeared that they had successfully modified their behavior. This also is a natural occurrence and after a spike in the wrong direction, the behavior will often correct and improve, and then stick in place. Don't panic, if you see either of these things happen. Stay the course and it will get better.

If you give up because it's easier, you are not doing your loved one any favors. If you want to see a change, you need to continue measuring all of your performance until you have made your new reality a habit.

* * *

To summarize, KPIs are a great tool for both monitoring improvements and holding everyone accountable to each other. Ideally, your KPIs should be placed on your Family Board for easy reference. You want to have them posted in a place where the family can easily see them and see your progress. The comments around the progress should always be positive and constructive, regardless of the direction of the progress. You should also consider reviewing your KPIs daily. For some KPIs, weekly might be appropriate. Whatever the cadence of the review, make sure you are consistent.

Let visual management work for you. You can use colors to indicate status, like green for good, yellow for warning, and red for bad. You can use a Harvey Ball, by shading in the quarters of the pie to indicate your level of completion. Use graphs and bar charts, spider diagrams, pie charts, tally marks, and anything else that will help you to visually understand where you are towards your goal.

I would recommend that a family not have any more than four KPIs at any given time, but three is probably a more manageable number. You want to be able to concentrate on doing a good job. If you add too many KPIs then nothing seems to get done. Remember to limit your WIP (Work in Progress). Plan on up to three things you want to work on as a family, and one personal KPI for each person to work on. We want to train our kids to work on their own self-improvement, as well as working as a team on the family and household goals.

**The steps for creating a KPI:**

**1.** Decide what you want to improve. Ideally, you have buy-in from the other family members involved to make this successful. Don't make the improvement an attack on an individual, it's never "you" need to fix this, but "we" will do this together.

**2.** Make the purpose of the KPI clear. Why are we doing this? What does success look like?

**3.** Agree on how to calculate or measure the KPI. What is your end goal?

**4.** Track and update the KPI regularly – this could be daily or weekly, but be consistent.

**5.** Discuss progress or lack of progress towards the KPI in your Family Board Meetings.

**6.** If you don't see any improvement, don't be afraid to update or tweak the KPI to fit your needs or change your approach to reach your KPI goal.

As you utilize family and personal KPIs into your routine, you will see steady improvement. You will see your children motivated, as they see their progress. The visual management of KPIs really does work wonders in helping you reach your goals.

You might consider simple incentives for your children as they are working toward achieving their goals to help keep them motivated. Rewards for hitting certain milestones also have their place. It is up to you to determine what is appropriate. In the end, as they see their progress, this will act as a motivating factor.

I only included this one tool in the EXPERIMENT Phase. While there are other tools that can be used in this phase, KPIs are the most important one. Just like a scientist performing an experiment, they measure their results. They adjust the experiment, if needed. And finally, they complete it.

In the previous phases you identified the problem in the GATHER Phase. You looked for the root cause and developed a roadmap with the solutions to the problem in the ASK Phase. In the TINKER Phase, you acted on the solutions you created.

In this phase, you are testing your hypothesis by creating KPIs around what you want to improve. You track the results to see that you are making progress. By having KPIs, you can see the results of your improvement plan. If it is working, you will continue to follow your plan. If you are not making progress on your roadmap to success, then you adjust your plan. You experiment to see what will make a difference. Thanks to KPIs, you can see what works and what doesn't, adjust your approach if needed, and continuously improve as a family.

*"If you would hit the mark,*
*you must aim a little above it:*
*Every arrow that flies feels the pull of the Earth."*
*- Henry Wadsworth Longfellow*

*"It must be borne in mind that the
tragedy of life doesn't lie in not reaching your goal.
The tragedy lies in having no goal to reach.
It isn't a calamity to die with dreams unfulfilled,
but it is a calamity not to dream.
It is not a disgrace not to reach the stars,
but it is a disgrace to have no stars to reach for.
Not failure, but low aim is a sin."*

*– Benjamin E. Mays*

# KPI 3x5 TEMPLATES

THESE ARE JUST SOME SAMPLE KPI TEMPLATES YOU CAN USE TO MONITOR CHANGES

TITLE:_____

|  | S | M | T | W | TH | F | S | TOTAL |
|---|---|---|---|---|---|---|---|---|
|  |  |  |  |  |  |  |  |  |
|  |  |  |  |  |  |  |  |  |
|  |  |  |  |  |  |  |  |  |
|  |  |  |  |  |  |  |  |  |
|  |  |  |  |  |  |  |  |  |
|  |  |  |  |  |  |  |  |  |

TITLE: _Weight Loss KPI_    MONTH: _____
GOAL: _____

TITLE:_____
GOAL:_____

LAST MONTH'S BILL: ☐

THIS MONTH'S GOAL: ☐

SAVINGS/LOSS

THIS MONTH'S ACTUAL: ☐  ☐

•◯• FamilyMBA

# SECTION 2:

## *The GATES™ Framework - SUSTAIN*

**OBJECTIVES:**

**1.** Maintain improvement gains by standardizing the new process improvement.

**2.** Celebrate successes and praise improvements through regular communication.

**3.** Continuous improvement is about starting the process over again.

# CHAPTER 17

## Definition of Done & Standard Work Sheets – Making Your Changes Stick

*The SUSTAIN Phase is all about taking the improvements you made and standardizing them to maintain your gains. It is essential to define what "done" looks like when making improvements.*

The first time I visited a manufacturing plant that effectively used the concept of visual management to help the workers perform their jobs I was blown away. I had never been there before, but the visual management directions were so good, I could have performed the job. These directions had such great illustrations that it was like following the step-by-step guide of an IKEA catalog. These directions are referred to as Standard Work Instructions and they are going to make your life at home easier. Especially when you introduce an element of the Standard Work Instructions known as the Definition of Done.

The business tools of the Standard Work Instructions and the Definition of Done are going to eliminate so many problems you have when trying to get the kids to do their chores or homework. It will also make the improvements you have been working on something that will stick and become part of a better family life.

In the SUSTAIN Phase, you are looking to make sure that the improvements and changes you have made stay in place and that your family doesn't backslide into the old habits you had before you made the changes. These two tools will help you make sure that you can sustain the changes you have made before you repeat the GATES™ framework over again to continuously improve.

## Definition of Done

There are two main difficulties that occur within families that these tools can help you eliminate: inconsistency and poor communication. These traits have the same effect as playing a game where the rules are constantly changing. It reminds me of the comic strip Calvin and Hobbes, by Bill Waterson, and that famous game Calvin Ball, where the only rule is that you can't play Calvin Ball the same way twice.

Within a family, inconsistency leads to feelings of frustration, betrayal, uneasiness, and a general sense of unfairness. Poor communication likewise leads to all those feelings as well. Here is where establishing a Definition of Done is going to make your life so much easier.

Let me give you an example from my home. In the past, my wife and I would ask the kids to "do the dishes," and the kids would generally oblige by "doing the dishes." To them this meant unload the dishes if they were clean, or load the dishes that were in the sink into the dishwasher. What it meant to us was for them to unload, load, wash the pots, clean the counters, put away the food.

You can probably see the conflict that would arise. The kids would do what they thought we asked them to do and then they decided that they were done. When we asked them to get back in and finish the job, we now became the bad guys. "The work is never done," "there's no satisfying you," "you only asked me to do the dishes," they would argue. The problem we had was that we had not established a definition for what "done" looks like. There was no consistency and, as a result, this led to hurt feelings, arguing, and nagging in the home. That all changed, for the most part, when we introduced the business concept of the Definition of Done to the family.

Before we implemented this tool, there was that inconsistency and undefined standards that led to conflict. When you create that common definition for what "done" looks like, both parent and child agree and understand what is expected. Then there is no confusion about where the finish line is for completion. When you don't have a Definition of Done, you are constantly moving the finish line and that is where problems arise.

My family started off by using it in the kitchen. First, we explained to the family that we were going to create a Definition of Done for various activities we do in the house. This seems basic, but it had a tremendous impact.

Next, get the kids involved in establishing what constitutes "done." This is the best way to get the kids to feel part of the finished process. When they help contribute to it, they take ownership for it. When doing this exercise, you might be surprised to find that the reason they don't do something, is because they don't know how to do it. This might only come out because you have included them in the process. Or you might also find that they feel that certain steps are not necessary in cleaning. This might be where you need to get creative to help establish a mutual understanding.

For example, my boys felt that unless they could smell their bathroom, they didn't need to clean it. Arguing was pointless, especially with teenagers. This called for something more drastic – the "gross out" factor. I went out and bought a black light. Yes, the ultimate in visual management. The black light reveals things that the eye can't see or the nose smell. I haven't had to ask them again to clean their bathroom since. They want to do it and they want to use the black light to check to see if they are done.

The toilet looked clean, but when we introduced the Definition of Done using a black light, everything changed. Our kids now knew what we wanted "clean" to look like and with that clear definition they knew how to do it.

This brings up a great point. When your kids help create and define what "done" looks like, then there is no arguing about if the job is done or not. As I mentioned, there were miscommunications with our kids every time we asked them to do the dishes. We decided to have the kids draft up the Definition of Done for the kitchen on their own. This is key, we had them write it down. When they finished, we added one additional item to their list and everyone was happy with the definition we all helped create.

Now when we ask them to do the dishes everyone is clear what needs to get done because they created the finish line. They are on a race to cross that line to be finished with their job and get onto the things they want to do. This also spurs creativity, because by knowing the purpose and the Definition of Done, they can create a faster, stress-free way to arrive at the finish line. It empowers them to get the job done.

From time to time, they will attempt to create short cuts and not do everything they know they need to do. When this happens, having a clearly defined Definition of Done written down is liberating for you as a parent because you don't have to argue or nag at them. Simply refer them to the expected standards which they helped create (if they are older), or which you have taught to them, (if they are younger). It creates a checklist for them, and they know what needs to get done.

No longer are you playing a game of Calvin Ball, because as a family you have now formalized the rules about what is expected. The rules are set. This creates order. Order brings harmony. This is what the SUSTAIN Phase is about, creating standards so that the improvements you make are sustainable.

### Standard Work Instructions

The other tool to make completing tasks easier for the family is have a step-by-step guide for them to know what to do from beginning to end, known as Standard Work Instructions. Every family has a signature dish that they cook the same way every time. The reason they have consistent, repeatable results is because they have a recipe.

The same is true for following any other process, for example cleaning. From getting out the cleaning supplies, to the steps for cleaning, and, of course, the putting away of the things they used. These instructions, recipe, or Standard Work Instructions, as we refer to them, along with your Definition of Done, will create order in your home.

If you need help with the Standard Work Instructions for household chores, the Internet is full of examples that can help you. From blogs, to Pinterest, to the manufacturers' websites, you should be able to easily find what you need to create your own Standard

Work Instructions. Having them written down takes the pressure off you as a parent for constantly telling your kids what to do.

What I have found is that the children who attend my workshops love having a Definition of Done, because it removes the inconsistency that drives them crazy. There is no more finishing the job and then having the parent add one more thing, and then one more thing, and so on, until the child has become frustrated and has lost trust in you as the parent. Creating a Definition of Done is creating a finish line that they know if they reach it, their job is done. Having the recipe to follow in the form of Standard Work Instructions takes the guess work out of completing tasks.

As your family problem solves through the GATES™ framework, you will develop new ways to do things. Write down your solutions so that the family can have the reliable results that will make your home life easier. This is the final 1% of completing your improvement transformation. When you have it documented, you are ensuring that your problem-solving efforts were not in vain. Standard Work Instructions, when used to cement the changes you've achieved, become the recipe to reliable, repeatable results.

# Standard Work Instruction Template
KEEP IT SIMPLE

TASK:_____ TOOLS:_____

GOAL:_____ RESPONSIBLE:_____

**1** ☐

**2** ☐

**3** ☐

_____
_____
_____

**4** ☐

**5** ☐

**6** ☐

_____
_____
_____

**7** ☐

**8** ☐

**9** ☐

_____
_____
_____

DEFINITION OF DONE:_____
_____

# CHAPTER 18

## Retrospectives, Family One-on-Ones, and Other Tools to Improve Communication

*The final Phase of the GATES™ System really isn't a final step. The SUSTAIN Phase is about cementing the progress you've made in your improvements and then starting over to improve the next thing. Bit by bit, your life will continue to be better today than it was yesterday.*

The previous chapter discussed the importance of making sure that change becomes ingrained in the new and improved way of doing things. This is achieved in two ways. The Definition of Done and the Standard Work Instructions are both systematic ways of making sure the new change is recorded, so you can see and know what to do. The other way to make sure change sticks is to communicate your Success Stories.

The Family Board Meeting is an important part of changing your family, but as you've come to realize, it doesn't give you a lot of time to communicate things more than just at a high-level. Things like prioritizing tasks, discussing issues, or leaving time for planning out the calendar in advance, aren't covered in the daily Family Board

Meeting because of the limited time allocated to it. You really need a way to communicate the improvement changes and discuss next steps.

Therefore, usually once a week we have a longer Planning/Improvement meeting. In business, we simply call this the Retrospective. At home, this used to be called Sunday Dinner. Keeping with the business theme, I'll call it the Family Retrospective.

### Family Retrospective

The meeting itself is for your family to discuss lessons learned, teach best practices, or even review how you are doing towards reaching your goals. It's a time to reflect on the week, what went well, what didn't go well, and what you could or should do differently next week. It is a time to also look forward into the coming week and do a high-level planning session and prioritize action steps. You can talk about what waste you can eliminate out of your household systems or the value you can add to help make things run faster and smoother. Basically, the Family Retrospective Meeting is for your family to take a little time, reflect, and get ready for the upcoming week.

You know, they say the definition of insanity is doing the same thing over and over again expecting different results. The Family Retrospective is a great tool to avoid getting into that kind of situation. The timing of this meeting is longer than the Family Board Meeting. Instead of 15 minutes, this meeting is around a half an hour, but you can take more time as needed. Again, Time Box it and ideally schedule it for the same time every week.

In the Family Retrospective you want to make sure that everyone can have their voice heard. To keep it simple, in our family everyone has about a five-minute block of time to discuss anything that they feel is important to bring up with the family. If it helps you to stay focused on what needs to be covered, you can create an agenda beforehand.

This meeting can be conducted sitting around the table, but occasionally we will have part of the meeting in a location to help all of us learn a new process improvement someone in the family developed. Following that Lean philosophy of Continuous Process Improvement, we want to make sure the whole family knows how to implement a new process. In this case, we will all move to the laundry room, the bathroom, or the kitchen, to learn the new Standard Work Instructions for that process improvement as part of the Family Retrospective.

Now that we have talked about what is covered, how long it should take, where to hold it, and the technical aspects of scheduling a Family Retrospective, let me introduce you to two exercises you can do during the meeting to capture what went well and what you can do to improve things at home.

**Generating Insights**

The first tool, Generating Insights, will help your family to get a better understanding of how the week went. Start by giving everyone two different colored post-it notes[xvi]. One will represent positive items from the week, the other - negative items that happened. To better remember what happened during the week, post the days of the week down on the table or on the wall, so you can align your items with the day.

Next, Time Block the activity and give everyone 2-3 minutes to write down all the positive things on one color, say, green, and all the negative items on yellow post-it notes. At the end of that Time Box, have everyone post their items under the day that it happened. What do you see? More green or more yellow? More issues on one day rather than on another? Look for trends to discuss.

Go around the room and ask each family member to explain what they liked and didn't like, what went well and what didn't go well. Again, Time Box this for one minute or so, per person. Finally, Time Box three minutes to pick one, two, or three things to work on in the coming week. I personally would try to keep it under three things to work on.

You might want to do a couple of things before you finish this activity: first, take a picture of the Generating Insights graphic that you just created; second, compare how many positive to negative items you had this week and compare them to the previous weeks. Are you getting any better? This could become a great KPI for your family. Are there more positive or negative comments? Track them over time as a KPI to see how you are trending. Are things moving in the right direction? And finally, add these new items you are going to be working to improve as a family to your Family Kanban Board to review every day next week.

### Focus On/Focus Off

Another tool you can use in your Family Retrospective is called Focus On/Focus Off[xvii]. Now, Focus On/Focus Off is just like it sounds and is very similar to the Generate Insights tool I just explained. At the end of the week, during the Family Retrospective, ask every member of the family to answer two simple questions: "In the upcoming week, what should we spend more time Focusing On?" And, "What should we take our Focus Off of this coming week?" It would be great if you demonstrated first.

These two things could be related. Say you had a disagreement during the Family Board Meeting. You might say that, "We should spend more time focusing on understanding what the other person is saying rather than trying to defend our position."

Or these could be two unrelated things. "We should focus on updating the board before the meetings. And we should take our focus off of wasting our time with TV and video games this week." Let everyone, come up with some suggestions of Focus On/Focus Off – and then select no more than three that as a family you plan on improving in the coming week. Add these to your Family Board as a daily reminder.

I don't know about you, but to me Focus On/Focus Off kind of sounds like something from the movie the Karate Kid [xviii], "wax on/wax off, sand the floor, paint the fence." And in a way, not only is this tool like that, but all these tools I have been showing you in this system are like that. Because Daniel-san didn't think that any of those chores Mr. Miyagi was asking him to do were helping him learn karate.

Perhaps you have felt the same way about some of the tools from Parenting the Lean Way. But just like Daniel quickly learned that those things Mr. Miyagi had shown him really did help him learn Karate and strengthen his muscles more than he realized, I know that as you use these tools, you too will see how they can benefit you and your children to improve your family life.

### Family One-on-Ones

The final tool I want to share with you is the Family One-on-One. This is probably the simplest of them all. The Family One-on-One is simply scheduling individual time between yourself and each family member. The time you spend together and the cadence are up to you. This is time for you and the family member in the One-on-One to really connect. Your job is to give your complete attention to the other family member. Talk about what they want to talk about. Do what they want to do. Actively listen to what they say. This is not a time for your agenda, or to discuss what you want, this is their time with you.

The One-on-One is a great business tool that I have taught to hundreds of managers in my consulting role. From a business stand point, the piece that makes this such an effective management tool is that a portion of the One-on-One time is reserved to discuss some action step, or some goal that the person is working on. The manger can provide their experience and guidance to help the other person to grow in their role.

The Family One-on-One does not need to be as formal as the business usage of it. Simply devoting a small portion of the time to help your child with things they need help with, or want to improve, can really add value to them. However, for this to be effective for your children, it needs to be something they request from you, not something you mandate. Use this time to mentor and coach your children, helping them to find their own solutions to the things they are working on, when they ask for it.

If you take time to have regular One-on-One time with your family members, your relationship with each of them will grow. Continuous improvement is great. Solving problems removes stress and worry, but spending quality time with each of your family members is priceless. There is nothing better than having special memories of the One-on-One time with each child and your spouse. They are why you do everything, so be sure to show your love to them. Treasure the time you have with them by taking time to have One-on-Ones. Before you realize it, your children will be grown and on their own, and you will wish you had taken the time.

My hope is that you will continue to use these tools to help you in your parenting and to strengthen the skill sets of your children as well. As you continue to practice these tools, they will become second nature. You will begin to see value and waste in everything. You will naturally look for *Kaizen*, or improvement opportunities. Continuous Family Improvement™ will become a way of life for you, and while using these tools and methods, you are going to find your family has been transformed. The stress is gone. The nagging and arguing will be replaced with teamwork and cooperation.

In the end, you are going to find that even though you might feel beat up, knocked down, and the odds might feel stacked against you as a parent, know that if you continue to use these tools, you will eventually find yourself winning the tournament of being a great parent.

Now that you have used the tools of Standard Work Instructions, the Definition of Done, and Family Retrospectives to sustain the improvements you have made, you need to start over again and gather the next thing your family wants to improve. The GATES™ framework is not a once and you're done system, but a continuous improvement process that creates accountability for the whole family. Parenting the Lean Way is about empowering you and your family to share your best selves with each other and the world, by proactively recognizing opportunities and developing solutions. When you and your family have a Continuous Family Improvement™ mindset, life will get better day by day.

JARED E. THATCHER

# SECTION 3:

## *CONCLUSION*

# CHAPTER 19

## Final Thoughts – This is Just the First Step

*Parenting the Lean Way is about working together on Continuous Family Improvement™. It may not be easy today, but stay the course and you will have joy in your transformations. Make the journey fun, and your family will grow stronger together.*

Parents have been struggling with raising kids for millenniums and, in that sense, there is nothing new in our challenge today as parents. However, because of recent technological advancements, we are the first generation of parents to deal with unique challenges that our parents never had to face—we don't have the example of the generation before us to show us how to deal with these new challenges. Thanks to the prevalence, addictive nature, and the instantenous and easy access to technology, our children experience challenges that we didn't face when we were their age.

While I haven't addressed these topics directly, I have provided you with a framework to be able to address these and other problems together as a family. The GATES™ framework can help you improve your communication as a family and work together to solve problems and challenges. Use these Lean tools to move you forward to identify the problem, understand the root cause, develop and try solutions, measure your results, celebrate your successes, and then take the next step to start over and improve it even more. Remember: Gather, Ask, Tinker, Experiment, Sustain – follow these five simple steps to improve your life.

But there is another benefit that comes from using business tools and methods in the home, and that is improved executive functioning skills. Executive functions are the skills we all need to get things done. These skills are controlled by three types of brain functions: working memory, mental flexibility, and self-control. None of us are born with these skills, we all must learn them.

What a priceless advantage you are giving to your children by showing them how to critically think and solve problems. Through these tools you are also teaching them to prioritize, plan, communicate, initiate tasks without supervision, recognize roadblocks, figure out workarounds, and to set and reach their goals. These are just a few of the executive functioning skills that you can learn to strengthen from using the business tools and methods outlined in Parenting the Lean Way.

Can you imagine the successes your children will experience in life by using these tools and methods? Can you envision how these tools can help improve your home life? If you have been using them while reading this book, then I know that you are starting to experience some of the successes they can bring to your life. Imagine also the potential success you can have in your own profession by using these tools in your career, or your children using them as they begin to work?

These tools will not only help your family to improve, but they will also help your school-age children as they transition into adulthood. Let me offer one more example. One of my teenage sons had an argument with his Mom when she asked him to put something away that had been left out for over a week after a camping trip. A short time later when she asked him again to do it, he got upset.

Unbeknownst to my wife, he had left the room to get the case to put the object away. She thought he was ignoring her, which is why she asked him if he was going to do it. He felt he was being picked on and micro-managed, even though he was doing what she had asked. This led to the misunderstanding.

I stepped in and stopped the argument that was starting to brew.

The next day, I made him sit down with his mother and complete a few business problem-solving tools. These were basic tools, but the first time he had ever used them. Once my wife and son started to work on them, they began to laugh and enjoy it. As he worked through these problem-solving tools, they expanded his understanding of the situation. He saw things from his mother's perspective.

He realized this. It wasn't his Mom telling him. It was him doing the work to understand why the argument had happened. Through these business tools, he saw the situation from a new perspective. He identified the root causes behind the argument. He came to his own conclusion. He had a paradigm shift.

My son approached me. "Dad, I hate to admit it, but I was responsible for the argument. I thought it was Mom, but I started it. If I had simply told her what I was about to do, this whole thing could have been avoided."

I don't know too many teenagers that would ever admit that they were in the wrong. This is what Parenting the Lean Way can do for you. It provides tools to help improve your family. It reduces stress and creates harmony in the home. Communication improves, processes improve, and relationships strengthen. That's powerful.

\* \* \*

Inside our home, we have grown closer together as a family by using these tools and methods. We communicate better as a family. We have become less critical of each other and work together to get things done. The kids have greater trust in us as their parents, because they know we value their opinion and they feel empowered to make decisions that help us out.

We are pleased with the responsibilities they have been taking on. Chores are done without complaining (most of the time), and the kids take initiative for identifying things they would like to make improvements on.

Keeping the Family Board Meetings and the Family Retrospective a safe place without criticism creates positive engagement, recognition, laughter, and builds closer relationships with the family.

Parenting the Lean Way helps greatly reduce nagging, as children understand the purpose, the Definition of Done is clear, and accountability is created through visual management. The Family Board plays a significant role in bringing all the tools discussed in this book together to empower the parents and the kids.

For the last several years, I have been doing workshops with families and friends, and it was on their suggestions that I decided to move these tools to the next level. This book is a piece of that puzzle.

I have provided you with over two dozen business tools and concepts, but these are by no means a complete list of business tools, frameworks, or methodologies. There are hundreds of them in use today. Not all have application within the family, but when it comes to soft skill development from the business world, I haven't even scratched the surface. These are the tools and competencies that will help both parents and kids.

There are several things in my online course "Parenting the Lean Way™" that are not found in this book. That course goes into greater depth, with more examples and tools. If you like the concepts found in this book, then I know you will be excited to learn more from that course. For less than the price of a video gaming system, you will begin seeing an almost instant return on your investment in the improvements in your family life from that course. For the improved harmony and reduced stress alone, it's worth it.

For those of you interested in my Parenting the Lean Way™ course, my workshops, private coaching, or our summer and winter week-long family retreat programs, you can find out more information at www.familymba.com

I would love to hear the feedback from each of you. Please take a moment to leave a review of this book where you purchased the book. I plan on putting future versions of this book through the GATES™ system. I want to understand your needs, so that I can provide those things that would be of the most value to you. Just like my parenting skills, I want to continuously be improving this book, my courses, my coaching, and my workshops and retreats.

Follow me on Facebook at: fb.me/ParentingTheLeanWay. When you like and follow the page you will find an incredible community of like-minded parents eager to learn more about the Lean Way™. You can register for my free newsletter to get regular tips and tools to help you improve your parenting. Plus, you can ask me questions directly. I would love to hear your success stories about your adventures in Parenting the Lean Way. Your feedback about the book or the tools, and any questions you might have will be answered on that site.

As a special thank you for following my book page and hopefully leaving a review of this book, I want to provide you with a free audio of this book. You can request your free audio book from the book website: http://www.ParentingTheLeanWay.com/Audio

It is my hope that you found things of value in this book to help you improve your parenting skills. You need not be on this journey alone. Together as parents we can learn and share helpful tools and hints to help strengthen our parenting abilities. I would hope that as you learn useful things from this book, that you will share what you have learned with others about Parenting the Lean Way so that they too can enjoy a lifestyle of Continuous Family Improvement™.

Until next time, continuously improve your life.

*"That which we persist in doing becomes easier to do,*
*not that the nature of the thing has changed*
*but that our power to do has increased."*
*- Ralph Waldo Emerson*

# APPENDIX

## *Worksheet Templates*

To download the Parenting the Lean Way templates found in this book, visit:

www.ParentingTheLeanWay.com/Templates

# VISUAL IDEA CUE CARDS

## VISUAL IDEA CUE CARDS 1/9

## VISUAL IDEA CUE CARDS 2/9

## VISUAL IDEA CUE CARDS 3/9

## VISUAL IDEA CUE CARDS 4/9

## VISUAL IDEA CUE CARDS 5/9

## VISUAL IDEA CUE CARDS 6/9

## VISUAL IDEA CUE CARDS 7/9

## VISUAL IDEA CUE CARDS 8/9

## VISUAL IDEA CUE CARDS 9/9

# PARENTING
## THE LEAN WAY

# ABOUT THE AUTHOR

Jared E. Thatcher is the world's leading expert on Lean Parenting™, his advice and business parenting tools are used by parents in over 130 countries. He has lectured all over the world and speaks three languages. He is a management consultant working with international charities, fortune 500 companies, government agencies, and small businesses, helping them solve problems, analyze data, and implement Lean into their organizations. He earned his MBA in International Business from the University of Edinburgh in Scotland, which included study at EADA Business School in Barcelona, Spain. He has his Lean Bronze Certification (LBC) from the Society of Manufacturing Engineers, is a Certified Scrum Master (CSM), and has his Project Management Professional (PMP) certification. An eighth generation Oregonian, Jared lives outside of Portland, Oregon with his wife and four children. They love spending time outdoors and enjoying all the beauty the Pacific Northwest has to offer.

# END NOTES:

i Victor C.X. Wang, Kathleen P. King, Building Workforce Competencies in Career and Technical Education, (Information Age Publishing, Inc., 2009), 161.

ii https://www.trainingindustry.com/blog/outsourcing/how-big-is-the-training-market/

iii The Natural Resources Defense Council (NRDC) Issue Paper August 2012 (pg.12): https://www.nrdc.org/sites/default/files/ wasted-food-IP.pdf

iv Stephen R. Covey, The 7 Habits of Highly Effective People, (New York, A Fireside Book, 1990), pg. 31.

v Charles Darwin, Letter to his sister Susan Elizabeth Darwin (4 August 1836). As quoted in: The Life and Letters of Charles Darwin (1887), volume I, chapter VI: "The Voyage", page 266.

vi Jared E. Thatcher, "The Family Envision Workshop", 20 August 2016, Tualatin, Oregon.

vii Taiichi Ohno, Workplace Management, (New York: McGraw-Hill Companies, 2009), 175

viii The Natural Resources Defense Council (NRDC) Issue Paper August 2012 (pg.12): https://www.nrdc.org/sites/default/files/ wasted-food-IP.pdf

ix http://smallplatemovement.org/wp-content/uploads/2017/06/
portion_size_me_JADA_2007.pdf

x https://www.thefactsite.com/2010/03/how-much-time-people-spend-doing
-stuff.html

xi http://www.apa.org/research/action/multitask.aspx

xii Jeanie Daniel Duck, The Change Monster, (New York: Three Rivers Press,
2001)

xiii Peter Hill, Concepts of Coaching: A Guide for Managers, (Oxford: Chandos
Publishing Limited, 2004), 186

xiv http://www.redcrowmarketing.com/2015/09/10/many-ads-see-one-day/

xv Bruce Feiler, "The Stories the Bind Us," New York Times, 17 March 2013, ST1

xvi Pieter Jongerius, et al., GET AGILE! Scrum for UX, Design & Development,
(Amsterdam: BIS Publishers, 2014), 107.

xvii Esther Derby & Diana Larsen, Agile Retrospectives: Making Good Teams
Great, (Raleigh: The Pragmatic Bookshelf, 2006), 44.

xviii Karate Kid, Directed by John G. Avildsen, 126 min., Columbia Pictures
Corporation, 1984.

# INDEX

# PARENTING
## THE LEAN WAY

# BONUS MATERIAL

## Thank You for Purchasing my eBook

I really appreciate you buying my book, and since you took action, I am going to give you my audiobook version for FREE! To download, visit:

### http://www.ParentingTheLeanWay.com/audio

To learn more about Parenting the Lean Way,
to ask me questions,
and get helpful tips,
please Like and Follow the book on FaceBook at:

### fb.me/ParentingTheLeanWay

## Now I have one favor to ask of you. . .

. . .Please take the time to leave a review of this book
with the retailer where you purchased it.
Your review will help other parents find this resource.
**Thank You!!!**

Printed in Great Britain
by Amazon